TRIVIA TEAM PUBLISHING

The Ultimate Serial Killer Trivia Book

Contents

I   The Ultimate Serial Killer Trivia Book

Introduction   3
How to Use This Book   5

II   Trivia Questions

Luis Garavito   9
Enriqueta Martí   11
Boston Strangler   12
Peter Sutcliffe   14
Arthur Shawcross   15
Belle Gunness   17
Carl Eugene Watts   19
Monster of Florence   21
Lee Choon-jae   23
Maurizio Minghella   25
Pedro López   27
Ted Bundy   29
Chester Turner   31
Jack the Ripper   32
Donald Henry Gaskins   34
Charles Ray Hatcher   35
Jeffrey Dahmer   37
Randy Kraft   38

Robert Hansen 40

Richard Cottingham 41

Randall Woodfield 43

Larry Eyler 44

Francisco Guerrero Pérez 45

Javed Iqbal 46

Mikhail Popkov 47

Daniel Camargo Barbosa 48

Pedro Rodrigues Filho 49

Hoshang Amini 50

Yang Xinhai 51

Samuel Little 52

William Unek 54

Mohammed Bijeh 55

Andrei Chikatilo 56

Anatoly Onoprienko 58

Florisvaldo de Oliveira 60

Gary Ridgway 61

Alexander Pichushkin 63

Ahmad Suradji 65

Raman Raghav 66

Moses Sithole 67

Gennady Mikhasevich 68

Vera Renczi 69

Fernando Hernández Leyva 70

John Wayne Gacy 71

Ali Asghar Borujerdi 73

Vasili Komaroff 74

Radik Tagirov 75

Karl Denke 76

Monster of the Mangones 77

Milton Sipalo 78

Zhang Jun 79

Mariam Soulakiotis 81

Cedric Maake 83

Robert Pickton 84

Bruce George Peter Lee 86

The Stoneman 87

Juan Corona 88

Fritz Haarmann 89

Béla Kiss 91

Yvan Keller 92

Ronald Dominique 93

Juan Fernando Hermosa 95

Earle Nelson 96

Patrick Kearney 98

William Bonin 99

III Answer Key

Luis Garavito 103

Enriqueta Martí 104

Boston Strangler 105

Peter Sutcliffe 106

Arthur Shawcross 107

Belle Gunness 108

Carl Eugene Watts 109

Monster of Florence 110

Lee Choon-jae 112

Maurizio Minghella 113

Pedro López 114

Ted Bundy 115

Chester Turner 117

Jack the Ripper 118

Donald Henry Gaskins 119

Charles Ray Hatcher 120

Jeffrey Dahmer	121
Randy Kraft	122
Robert Hansen	123
Richard Cottingham	124
Randall Woodfield	125
Larry Eyler	126
Francisco Guerrero Pérez	127
Javed Iqbal	128
Mikhail Popkov	129
Daniel Camargo Barbosa	130
Pedro Rodrigues Filho	131
Hoshang Amini	132
Yang Xinhai	133
Samuel Little	134
William Unek	135
Mohammed Bijeh	136
Andrei Chikatilo	137
Anatoly Onoprienko	138
Florisvaldo de Oliveira	139
Gary Ridgway	140
Alexander Pichushkin	142
Ahmad Suradji	143
Raman Raghav	144
Moses Sithole	145
Gennady Mikhasevich	146
Vera Renczi	147
Fernando Hernández Leyva	148
John Wayne Gacy	149
Ali Asghar Borujerdi	150
Vasili Komaroff	151
Radik Tagirov	152
Karl Denke	153
Monster of the Mangones	154

Milton Sipalo	155
Zhang Jun	157
Mariam Soulakiotis	158
Cedric Maake	159
Robert Pickton	160
Bruce George Peter Lee	161
The Stoneman	162
Juan Corona	163
Fritz Haarmann	164
Béla Kiss	166
Yvan Keller	167
Ronald Dominique	168
Juan Fernando Hermosa	170
Earle Nelson	171
Patrick Kearney	172
William Bonin	173

I

The Ultimate Serial Killer Trivia Book

Introduction

Serial killers have long fascinated the public's mind, holding a dark and chilly corner in human history. Their stories, combining moments of horror and fascination, unmask the extreme level of human behavior, where the last frontiers of one's twisted mind turn the most unspeakable fantasies into grim reality. Still, despite the cruelty of their deeds, we are still captivated by our interest in what brings individuals to such cruelty. Is it possible for nature or nurture to be the explanation? What types of behavioral patterns and psychological features characterize them? Those questions tease and tantalize criminologists, psychologists, and the public in general, making serial killers a gruesome yet fascinating subject to study.

This trivia book takes the reader on a journey through history's most infamous cases of serial murderers-from 19th-century London's most notorious, Jack the Ripper, to the modern-day predators whose acts of violence shook whole nations. These pages are packed full of amazing facts, chilling details, and lesser-known insight into the lives of these killers to shed light on their methods, motives, and, in some instances, even their eventual downfall. In this tour, we profess not only to gaze at the crime but to provide an understanding of the societal, psychological, and historical contexts that mold such monstrous figures.

Dive in to reveal some of the most unbelievable, many times horrific, truths from behind the mask of some of the world's deadliest individuals. It is more than a trivia book on gore and guts; it is also one that acts as a memorial to the dark side of human nature and vigilance, justice, and compassion that could help in the avoidance of such tragedies in the future. Embark upon a voyage into the serial killer's brain. Get ready for both horror and fascination.

How to Use This Book

This book is going to test your knowledge, taking you through a dark world of serial killers. If you're studying for your own sake or having some fun with friends over trivia night, these pages have hours of exciting content in store. Here's a quick breakdown of what you can expect from this book:

The following chapter contains trivia-type questions, which are categorized by topic. That is, each chapter addresses one category in particular to help you focus on those specific elements of serial killers that interest you the most. You can read these in any order if you like; go directly to the topic that capture your curiosity.

The final section contains the answer key. The answers are in the same order as the questions so as not to spoil anything. Once you've conquered this subject, don't forget to check out our other books in the series for more riveting trivia!

II

Trivia Questions

Luis Garavito

1. What was Luis Alfredo Garavito's nickname, which translates to "The Beast" in English?
2. In which country did Garavito commit most of his murders?
3. How many victims did Garavito confess to sexually assaulting and murdering between 1992 and 1999?
4. What year was Garavito apprehended by the police?
5. How long was Garavito's original sentence in prison, according to the court ruling?
6. What was the maximum number of years Colombian law allows for imprisonment?
7. What condition did Garavito suffer from that affected his vision?
8. Which two personality disorders were psychiatrists said to have diagnosed Garavito with?
9. In which country did Garavito reportedly murder four additional victims in 1998?
10. Garavito often wore disguises while committing his crimes. Name two of the disguises he used.
11. What did Garavito reportedly write in after committing each of his crimes?
12. What substance did Garavito frequently consume near school zones before targeting his victims?
13. What physical object did police find at a crime scene that helped them identify Garavito?

14. In which year did Garavito die, and at what age?
15. Which journalist interviewed Garavito for a show broadcast in 2006?

Enriqueta Martí

1. In what year was Enriqueta Martí born?
2. What was Enriqueta Martí's nickname in the press?
3. What was the name of the young girl Martí was proven to have abducted?
4. In what city did Martí open her own brothel in 1909?
5. What type of clients did Martí's brothel cater to?
6. What did Martí claim could cure tuberculosis?
7. How did Martí dispose of her victims' remains?
8. During which significant event was Martí arrested in 1909, but not tried?
9. What was the name of the neighbor who helped identify Martí's last victim, Teresita Guitart?
10. What did the police find inside Martí's flat at 29 carrer Ponent in 1912?
11. Who was the little boy Angelita claimed Martí killed in her flat?
12. What excuse did Martí give to explain the disappearance of Pepito, the young boy Angelita mentioned?
13. Where did Martí claim to have taken Angelita from?
14. How did Martí die in prison?
15. What cause of death was listed on Martí's death certificate?
16. According to historian Elsa Plaza, what were the bones found in Martí's flat determined to belong to?
17. What did some historians suggest about Martí's role as a scapegoat for the upper class?

Boston Strangler

1. Who was the main suspect in the Boston Strangler murders?
2. How many women were murdered by the Boston Strangler between June 1962 and January 1964?
3. What nickname was initially used for the murderer before "The Boston Strangler" became common?
4. What was the name of the attorney who defended Albert DeSalvo in court?
5. Who helped coordinate the various police forces investigating the murders?
6. What controversial method did Attorney General Edward W. Brooke use to help investigate the murders?
7. What pseudonyms was Albert DeSalvo known by for his earlier crimes?
8. In what year was Albert DeSalvo sentenced to life in prison?
9. What happened to DeSalvo after he escaped from Bridgewater State Hospital in 1967?
10. Who was the final victim linked to the Boston Strangler?
11. What evidence in 2013 conclusively linked DeSalvo to the final victim?
12. What theory did Dr. Ames Robey, a medical director, propose about DeSalvo's role in the murders?
13. What did former FBI profiler Robert Ressler argue about the Boston Strangler case?
14. Who took up the cause of the DeSalvo family to clear his name in the year 2000?

15. How did forensic pathologist Michael Baden challenge DeSalvo's con-
    fession regarding Mary Sullivan's murder?

Peter Sutcliffe

1. What was Peter Sutcliffe's alias in the press?
2. How many women was Sutcliffe convicted of murdering?
3. When was Sutcliffe arrested?
4. What did Sutcliffe claim inspired him to kill?
5. What was the name of Sutcliffe's first murder victim?
6. Where did two of Sutcliffe's murders take place outside of West Yorkshire?
7. What psychological condition was Sutcliffe diagnosed with in 1984?
8. Who conducted a review of the investigation after Sutcliffe's conviction, which led to changes in UK police procedures?
9. How many times did police interview Sutcliffe before his arrest?
10. In what year was Sutcliffe transferred to HM Prison Frankland?
11. Who was the youngest murder victim of Sutcliffe?
12. What weapon did Sutcliffe commonly use in his attacks?
13. What nickname was given to the hoaxer who sent misleading letters and a tape during the investigation?
14. What significant police failure was highlighted in the review following Sutcliffe's conviction?
15. What was Sutcliffe's occupation before his arrest?

Arthur Shawcross

1. What was the nickname given to Arthur John Shawcross?
2. Where did Shawcross commit his first known murders?
3. How long did Shawcross serve in prison for his initial manslaughter plea?
4. What was Shawcross's occupation when he committed most of his murders in the late 1980s?
5. How old was Shawcross when he died, and where was he serving his prison sentence at the time?
6. Which psychiatrist described Shawcross as "one of the most egregious examples of the unwarranted release of a prisoner"?
7. In what branch of the military did Shawcross serve, and in what division?
8. How long did Shawcross serve in the Army before being discharged?
9. What disturbing behavior did Shawcross's second wife notice that concerned her?
10. What crimes did Shawcross commit after being released from his Army service and before his first known murders?
11. What plea deal was Shawcross allowed to take for his murders in 1972, and why was this deal offered?
12. How many years was Shawcross in prison before being granted early parole?
13. What psychological disorders were presented by Shawcross's defense during his 1990 trial?
14. Who refuted Shawcross's claims of post-traumatic stress from wartime

atrocities, and what did they conclude about him?

15. What was discovered about Shawcross's brain after his trial?

16. In what year was Shawcross interviewed about his claims of cannibalism, and how many victims did he claim to have eaten parts of?

Belle Gunness

1. What name was Belle Gunness born with?
2. In which two U.S. states was Belle Gunness active as a serial killer?
3. How many murders is Belle Gunness thought to have committed, according to the most conservative estimates?
4. How did Belle Gunness seemingly die?
5. What was Belle Gunness's occupation before she became infamous as a serial killer?
6. Who was Belle Gunness's first husband?
7. What happened to Belle Gunness's candy store and house during her first marriage?
8. How did Mads Sørensen, Belle Gunness's first husband, die?
9. What major purchase did Belle Gunness make with the life insurance money after her first husband's death?
10. How did Belle Gunness explain the death of her second husband, Peter Gunness?
11. What year did Belle Gunness start placing marriage ads in Chicago newspapers?
12. Which discovery in 1908 exposed Belle Gunness's criminal activities?
13. How many bodies were initially found on Belle Gunness's property after the fire?
14. Who was Ray Lamphere in relation to Belle Gunness?
15. What did Ray Lamphere confess to regarding Belle Gunness's scheme?
16. What inconsistencies were found in the headless body believed to be

Belle Gunness?

17. What was the result of the 2008 DNA test on the headless corpse?

18. Name one film inspired by Belle Gunness's life.

19. What is the title of the 2021 novel by Camilla Bruce based on Belle Gunness's life?

20. Which 2023 Norwegian novel provides a fictionalized account of Belle Gunness's life?

Carl Eugene Watts

1. What was Carl Eugene Watts' nickname?
2. What name was Carl Eugene Watts also known by in the media?
3. How many murders did Watts officially confess to?
4. How many victims did Watts later claim to have killed?
5. In what city and state was Carl Eugene Watts born?
6. What illness did Watts and his sister contract when he was 8 years old?
7. At what age did Watts reportedly begin having violent dreams about killing women?
8. How old was Watts when he first assaulted Joan Gave?
9. What was Watts diagnosed with during his time in psychiatric institutions?
10. In what year did Watts graduate from high school?
11. What sport did Watts excel in, earning him a scholarship to Lane College?
12. What was the name of Watts' first confirmed murder victim?
13. What nickname did newspapers give Watts due to his attacks taking place on Sunday mornings?
14. Which city's police arrested Watts after he attempted to attack Michele Maday, Melinda Aguilar, and Lori Lister?
15. What year was Watts sentenced to 60 years in prison?
16. In what year did Michigan authorities charge Watts for the murder of Helen Dutcher?
17. What was the outcome of Watts' trial for the murder of Western Michigan University student Gloria Steele?

18. What illness caused Carl Eugene Watts' death in 2007?

Monster of Florence

1. During what time period was the "Monster of Florence" active?
2. How many victims were attributed to the "Monster of Florence"?
3. What type of weapon was used in the murders?
4. What was unusual about the crime scenes involving female victims?
5. Who were the first victims of the Monster of Florence?
6. What nickname was given to Barbara Locci in her hometown?
7. What major development linked the 1968 murder to later crimes?
8. What disturbing detail was found regarding Stefania Pettini's body?
9. Why was Enzo Spalletti initially suspected of the murders?
10. Who were the victims of the 1983 murder that involved two male students?
11. What connection did the police draw between the Monster of Florence and a Satanic cult?
12. What did the anonymous caller suggest to the police after the murder of Stefano Baldi and Susanna Cambi?
13. What was the controversial evidence found in Pietro Pacciani's garden?
14. Who were the two men convicted after Pacciani's death?
15. What alleged motive did Lotti give for the murders in his changing testimonies?
16. What was the so-called "Sardinian trail" in the investigation?
17. Who was Francesco Narducci, and how was his death suspicious?
18. What role did journalist Mario Spezi play in the investigation?
19. Which 2017 investigation suggested a link between the Monster of

Florence and the Zodiac Killer?

20. Who was the main suspect in the connection between the Monster of Florence and the Zodiac Killer?

Lee Choon-jae

1. Who was Lee Chun-jae, and what is he infamous for committing?
2. In what province did Lee Chun-jae commit most of his crimes?
3. How many women and girls did Lee Chun-jae murder between 1986 and 1994?
4. What inspired the 2003 film *Memories of Murder*?
5. Why could Lee Chun-jae not be prosecuted for the Hwaseong serial murders despite confessing to them in 2019?
6. What event in Lee Chun-jae's childhood is believed to have traumatized him?
7. When did Lee Chun-jae join the Republic of Korea Army, and what role did he serve in?
8. What crime led to Lee Chun-jae's one-year-and-six-month prison sentence in 1989?
9. How many victims were murdered during the Hwaseong serial murders between 1986 and 1991?
10. How many man-days were spent investigating the Hwaseong serial murders?
11. What inaccurate detail about the killer's blood type was corrected in 2019?
12. Who was wrongfully convicted of one of the Hwaseong murders and later acquitted in 2020?
13. What strategy did the police employ using female officers to try to catch the serial killer?

14. How was Lee Chun-jae identified as a suspect in 2019?

15. What was Lee Chun-jae already serving a life sentence for when he was identified as the Hwaseong killer?

16. How many rapes and attempted rapes did Lee Chun-jae confess to in 2019?

17. Why was Lee Chun-jae not seeking parole and release, despite having the possibility of it?

18. What role did the film *Memories of Murder* play in keeping public interest in the Hwaseong case alive?

19. What evidence linked Lee Chun-jae to the Hwaseong murders in 2019?

20. What did the court find regarding the police treatment of Yoon Sung-yeo during his wrongful conviction?

Maurizio Minghella

1. In what city did Maurizio Minghella commit murders between 1997 and 2001 while on parole?
2. How many sex workers was Minghella sentenced for killing between 1997 and 2001?
3. How many women did Minghella kill in his hometown in 1978?
4. What nickname did Minghella receive due to his passion for disco music?
5. What was a traumatic event in Minghella's life that influenced his mental state?
6. What was Minghella's IQ as determined at the psychiatric clinic of the University of Genoa?
7. What year did Minghella marry 15-year-old Rosa Manfredi?
8. What was the name of the first prostitute Minghella killed in 1978?
9. How did Minghella try to mislead the investigation in his first murder?
10. What item linked Minghella to the murder of Maria Catena Alba?
11. Which two victims were friends and were killed by Minghella in 1978?
12. In what year was Minghella first sentenced to life imprisonment?
13. What job did Minghella do while in semi-liberty in 1995?
14. What object was used by Minghella to strangle 73-year-old Cosima "Gina" Guido in 1999?
15. What led to Minghella's second arrest in 2001?
16. How did Minghella attempt to escape from prison in 2001 and 2003?
17. In what year was Minghella sentenced to life imprisonment for the murder of Florentina Motoc?

18. In what prison is Maurizio Minghella currently serving his sentence?

Pedro López

1. What is the nickname of Pedro Alonso López?
2. In which country was Pedro Alonso López born?
3. How many siblings did Pedro Alonso López have?
4. What happened to López's father before he was born?
5. Why was Pedro Alonso López banished from his home at the age of eight?
6. At what age did López join a gang of street children?
7. In what year was Pedro Alonso López sentenced to prison for auto theft?
8. What crime did López commit against three inmates while in prison?
9. After his release from prison in 1978, which country did López travel to where he claimed to have killed over 100 girls?
10. What event led to López's arrest in 1980?
11. Who helped capture López after he attempted to abduct a young girl in Ecuador?
12. How did López lure his victims according to his confession?
13. How many confirmed victims were attributed to López in Ecuador?
14. What was the maximum prison sentence that López received in Ecuador in 1980?
15. When was López released from prison, and what was the reason given for his early release?
16. After being released from prison in Ecuador, which country deported López?
17. In what year was López declared sane and released on bail in Colombia?
18. When was the last reported sighting of Pedro Alonso López?

19. In what year did Guinness World Records stop listing Pedro Alonso López as the "most prolific serial killer"?

20. Which organization issued a warrant for López's arrest in 2002?

Ted Bundy

1. What was Ted Bundy's birth name?
2. How did Bundy typically lure his victims?
3. What did Bundy often do after killing his victims?
4. In what year was Bundy first arrested?
5. How many death sentences did Bundy receive for his Florida homicides?
6. Who characterized Bundy as a "sadistic sociopath"?
7. What did Bundy say about himself regarding his character?
8. Where was Bundy born?
9. Who raised Bundy during the first three years of his life?
10. What incident involving knives did Bundy's aunt Julia recall from his childhood?
11. What did Bundy's neighbors report about his behavior toward animals?
12. What was Bundy's only significant athletic activity in high school?
13. Where did Bundy study Chinese?
14. What organization did Bundy work for at the Suicide Hotline Crisis Center?
15. Who did Bundy rekindle a relationship with in 1973?
16. How did Bundy's relationship with Diane Edwards end?
17. What method did Bundy use in the murders of his early victims in 1974?
18. Which two women were abducted from Lake Sammamish State Park in July 1974?
19. What type of car did Bundy typically drive during his abductions?
20. What was significant about Bundy's escape from the Pitkin County

Courthouse in 1977?

21. What did Bundy do in the early hours of January 15, 1978, at Florida State University's Chi Omega sorority house?

22. What was Bundy's last known victim's name?

23. What method was used to execute Bundy in 1989?

24. What did Bundy confess to doing with some of his victims after their deaths?

25. How did Bundy alter his appearance to evade detection?

Chester Turner

1. What was Chester Dewayne Turner convicted of, and how many victims were involved?
2. What nickname was used for Turner before his identification as the killer?
3. In what year was Turner sentenced to death for his first set of murders?
4. Who was Turner's first confirmed murder victim, and when was her body found?
5. In which area did most of Turner's murders occur?
6. Which victim's murder in 1989 also involved the death of her unborn child?
7. Who was wrongfully convicted for some of the murders linked to Turner, and how long did he spend in prison?
8. How was Turner eventually linked to the murders he committed?
9. When was Turner convicted of four additional murders, and what was the outcome?
10. What happened regarding Turner's conviction for the murder of the unborn baby in 2020?
11. Where is Chester Dewayne Turner currently being held?

Jack the Ripper

1. In which district of London was Jack the Ripper active in 1888?
2. What other names was Jack the Ripper referred to in contemporaneous reports?
3. What type of knowledge did the removal of internal organs from at least three victims suggest the killer might have?
4. How did the name "Jack the Ripper" become known?
5. Which letter, received by George Lusk, came with half of a preserved human kidney?
6. What are the names of the five victims commonly referred to as the "canonical five"?
7. In what year did the first of the "Whitechapel murders" occur, according to the Metropolitan Police investigation?
8. What significant event occurred in the Whitechapel district between 1886 and 1889, heightening public unrest?
9. Who was the first victim of the "canonical five"?
10. What body part was missing from the crime scene of Mary Jane Kelly?
11. Who described seeing Annie Chapman in the company of a man on the morning of her murder?
12. Which two victims were killed in the "double event" on 30 September 1888?
13. What controversial message was found written near a piece of Catherine Eddowes's bloodied apron?
14. Which victim's body was discovered in the single room where she lived

at 13 Miller's Court?

15. What was the approximate population of Whitechapel in 1888?

16. How did the "From Hell" letter differ from the "Dear Boss" letter and "Saucy Jacky" postcard?

17. What was the reward offered by the Whitechapel Vigilance Committee for information leading to the capture of Jack the Ripper?

18. What term did Colin Wilson coin to describe the study and analysis of the Jack the Ripper case?

19. What profession was Jack the Ripper initially suspected of belonging to, due to the nature of the mutilations?

20. Which of the eleven Whitechapel murders occurred in 1891, after the canonical five?

Donald Henry Gaskins

1. What was the birth name of Donald Henry "Pee Wee" Gaskins Jr.?
2. How many people did Gaskins kill, according to his sworn testimony during his plea agreement?
3. How did police first discover the bodies near Gaskins' home in Prospect, South Carolina?
4. Who was Gaskins convicted of killing in 1976, leading to his initial death sentence?
5. In which prison did Gaskins commit the murder of fellow inmate Rudolph Tyner?
6. How did Gaskins kill Rudolph Tyner in 1982?
7. What was Gaskins' self-proclaimed number of murders before his execution, which was widely discredited?
8. What significant event led to Gaskins' final arrest in November 1975?
9. Who was Gaskins' first confirmed murder victim in November 1970?
10. What was the motive behind the murder of Doreen Dempsey and her daughter in 1973?
11. Who hired Gaskins to kill Silas Barnwell Yates in 1975, and for how much?
12. What nickname did Gaskins earn after committing another murder while already incarcerated?
13. How did Gaskins initially attempt to kill Tyner before using explosives?
14. What were Gaskins' last words before his execution in 1991?

Charles Ray Hatcher

1. Where was Charles Ray Hatcher born?
2. How many people did Hatcher confess to murdering between 1969 and 1982?
3. What tragic event occurred while Hatcher and his brothers were flying a kite in 1936?
4. What crime led to Hatcher's first conviction in 1947?
5. How many times was Hatcher sentenced to prison by 1959?
6. In 1959, who did Hatcher attempt to abduct in St. Joseph, Missouri?
7. What crime was Hatcher accused of committing in the Missouri State Penitentiary in 1961?
8. Who was Hatcher's first confessed murder victim in 1969?
9. Under what false name was Hatcher arrested in 1969 for the assault of Gilbert Martinez?
10. How did Hatcher try to avoid trial after being charged with the assault of Gilbert Martinez?
11. In what year did Hatcher escape from a mental hospital for the first time?
12. What was Hatcher diagnosed with by a psychiatrist in 1973?
13. What parole date was set for Hatcher after his good behavior in 1976?
14. What crime led to Hatcher's arrest in Omaha, Nebraska, in 1978?
15. Who was wrongfully convicted for the murder of Eric Christgen before Hatcher confessed?
16. What was the name of the 11-year-old girl murdered by Hatcher in 1982?
17. In what year did Hatcher confess to 15 other murders while awaiting

trial?

18. How did Charles Ray Hatcher die?

Jeffrey Dahmer

1. What nickname was Jeffrey Dahmer also known by?
2. How many males did Dahmer kill between 1978 and 1991?
3. Which mental disorders was Dahmer diagnosed with, despite being found legally sane?
4. In what year was Dahmer sentenced to life imprisonment for the murders he committed in Wisconsin?
5. What was Dahmer's first known murder victim's name?
6. Which prison inmate killed Dahmer in 1994?
7. In which state did Dahmer commit his first murder?
8. What was Dahmer's profession after being discharged from the army?
9. Where did Dahmer move after his discharge from the army?
10. What experiment did Dahmer attempt on his victims, involving drilling and injecting substances into their skulls?

Randy Kraft

1. What was Randy Kraft's nickname due to the list of victims found in his possession?
2. In which state did most of Kraft's murders occur?
3. What military branch did Randy Kraft serve in before being discharged?
4. What year was Randy Kraft arrested and formally charged with his first murder?
5. How many murders was Kraft convicted of committing between 1972 and 1983?
6. What was the primary method of murder used by Randy Kraft?
7. What led investigators to nickname Kraft the "Freeway Killer"?
8. Which political party did Kraft initially support before shifting his views in college?
9. How many coded entries were found on Kraft's "scorecard"?
10. What was the outcome of Kraft's trial in 1989?
11. In which prison is Randy Kraft currently incarcerated?
12. Who was Kraft's partner during the lull in murders from 1976 to 1979?
13. What evidence linked Kraft to the murder of Marine Robert Loggins in 1980?
14. What was the most expensive trial in Orange County history, lasting thirteen months?
15. What unusual evidence did investigators find at several crime scenes that suggested Kraft had an accomplice?
16. What did investigators find in Kraft's Toyota Celica that linked him to

multiple victims?

17. Who was Kraft's suspected accomplice in some of his murders between 1971 and 1976?

18. What other two serial killers were also known as the "Freeway Killer"?

Robert Hansen

1. What was Robert Hansen's nickname?
2. How many women did Robert Hansen abduct, rape, and murder?
3. In what year was Robert Hansen captured?
4. How many years of imprisonment was Robert Hansen sentenced to?
5. Where was Robert Hansen born?
6. What were some of Robert Hansen's characteristics in his youth?
7. In what year did Hansen enlist in the United States Army Reserve?
8. What crime led to Hansen's first major arrest in 1960?
9. What mental health diagnosis was Hansen given during his time in prison?
10. When did Hansen move to Anchorage, Alaska?
11. How many children did Hansen have with his second wife?
12. What weapon did Hansen often use to hunt his victims?
13. Who was believed to be Hansen's first murder victim, although he denied involvement?
14. What did Cindy Paulson do to escape from Hansen in 1983?
15. What crucial evidence did Cindy Paulson leave behind in Hansen's car?
16. What were some of the items found in Hansen's home during the search that helped convict him?
17. How many little "x" marks were found on Hansen's aeronautical chart?
18. Who created the FBI profile that helped track Hansen?
19. What was the plea bargain Hansen agreed to after his arrest?
20. How many grave sites did Hansen reveal to investigators?

Richard Cottingham

1. What nickname did the media give Richard Cottingham based on some of his murders?
2. How many murders was Richard Cottingham convicted of in New York and New Jersey combined?
3. In what year did Cottingham claim to have committed at least 80 "perfect murders"?
4. What job did Richard Cottingham hold at Blue Cross Blue Shield until his 1980 arrest?
5. How many children did Cottingham have with his wife before they divorced?
6. What weapons and tools did Cottingham possess when he was arrested in 1980?
7. Which motel did Cottingham take 18-year-old Leslie Ann O'Dell to, where he was arrested?
8. What did Cottingham allegedly tell Leslie Ann O'Dell during her assault?
9. What kind of personal effects were found in Cottingham's locked room after his 1980 arrest?
10. What did Cottingham do to 19-year-old prostitute Susan Geiger when he tortured her at the Airport Motel?
11. How did Cottingham murder Maryann Carr and where was her body found?
12. What evidence linked Cottingham to the murder of Valerie Ann Street at the Quality Inn in 1980?

13. Which hotel in New York City did firefighters discover two decapitated bodies on December 2, 1979?

14. How did Richard Cottingham dispose of Mary Ann Jean Reyner's body after killing her in 1980?

15. What method did Cottingham use to murder 17-year-old Lorraine Marie Kelly and Mary Ann Pryor in 1974?

16. Which cold case murder did Cottingham confess to in 2021, shortly before detective Robert Anzilotti's retirement?

17. Which unsolved double-homicide from 1974 did Cottingham admit to committing in April 2021?

18. In what year did Cottingham plead guilty to the murder of Diane Martin Cusick, solved through DNA evidence?

19. Who was Cottingham's 17-year-old victim found strangled in the Passaic River in 1967?

Randall Woodfield

1. What nickname was Randall Brent Woodfield given by the media?
2. How many murders has Woodfield been linked to, and how many is he suspected of committing?
3. What sport did Woodfield play, and which NFL team drafted him in 1974?
4. In what year was Woodfield arrested for indecent exposure while still in high school?
5. How did Woodfield commit his robberies and sexual assaults on women in Portland in 1975?
6. Who was Woodfield's earliest-documented murder victim, and when did it occur?
7. What sentence did Woodfield receive after his conviction for the murder of Shari Hull and the attempted murder of Beth Wilmot?
8. In which state is Woodfield currently incarcerated?
9. Where did Woodfield grow up, and what sport did he excel in during high school?
10. How many times has Woodfield been married while in prison?
11. What is one distinctive feature Woodfield used to disguise himself during his crimes?
12. In what year was Woodfield first convicted of murder, and who was the prosecutor during the case?

Larry Eyler

1. What nickname was Larry Eyler known by, due to where many of his victims were discovered?
2. In what years did Eyler commit his series of murders?
3. What was the primary method Eyler used to kill his victims?
4. What did Larry Eyler offer to confess to in exchange for commuting his death sentence to life imprisonment without parole?
5. What was Larry Eyler's cause of death while on death row?
6. Who was Eyler's alleged accomplice in several of his murders, according to Eyler?
7. How did Larry Eyler frequently dispose of his victims' bodies?
8. What was the name of the 16-year-old victim Eyler was convicted of murdering in 1984?
9. Which attorney represented Eyler and released his posthumous confession?
10. What object found in Eyler's apartment connected him to the murder of Daniel Bridges?

Francisco Guerrero Pérez

1. What was Francisco Guerrero Pérez's nickname?
2. How many women did Francisco Guerrero Pérez kill between 1880 and 1888?
3. In which Mexican city did Francisco Guerrero commit his murders?
4. What was Francisco Guerrero Pérez's profession?
5. How did Francisco Guerrero Pérez typically murder his victims?
6. What was the main motive behind Francisco Guerrero Pérez's murders?
7. Who arrested Francisco Guerrero Pérez for the first time?
8. What was Francisco Guerrero Pérez convicted of in his first trial?
9. What was Francisco Guerrero Pérez's original sentence for his first conviction, and who intervened to change it?
10. When was Francisco Guerrero Pérez released from prison after his first conviction?
11. For what crime was Francisco Guerrero Pérez arrested in 1908?
12. How did the authorities catch Francisco Guerrero Pérez after his final murder?
13. Where did Francisco Guerrero Pérez spend the last years of his life?
14. What was the likely cause of Francisco Guerrero Pérez's hatred toward women?
15. How did Francisco Guerrero Pérez die?

Javed Iqbal

1. What was Javed Iqbal Mughal's primary motive for committing the murders?
2. In what year did Javed Iqbal confess to the murder of 100 young boys?
3. What method did Javed Iqbal use to dispose of the bodies of his victims?
4. How old were most of Javed Iqbal's victims?
5. What item did police find in Javed Iqbal's house that helped confirm his crimes?
6. What event in Javed Iqbal's life did he claim led him to commit his murders?
7. How did Javed Iqbal reportedly die in jail?
8. Where did Javed Iqbal turn himself in after being on the run from police?
9. What sentence was Javed Iqbal given by the judge after being convicted?
10. What was the name of the film based on Javed Iqbal's story, and when was it finally released?

Mikhail Popkov

1. What is the nickname given to Mikhail Popkov due to the brutal nature of his crimes?
2. How many murders did Mikhail Popkov confess to in total?
3. In which two Russian regions did Mikhail Popkov primarily commit his crimes?
4. What occupation did Mikhail Popkov hold before being arrested for his crimes?
5. When was Mikhail Popkov first convicted of 22 murders?
6. What significant clue led to Mikhail Popkov's capture?
7. What was Mikhail Popkov's stated motive for his murders?
8. What tools did Mikhail Popkov use to kill his victims?
9. What year did Mikhail Popkov receive a second life sentence after confessing to more murders?
10. How many additional killings did Mikhail Popkov confess to in July 2020?
11. Who did Mikhail Popkov falsely accuse of infidelity, contributing to his violent behavior?
12. How many additional years in prison was Mikhail Popkov sentenced to in 2021 after being found guilty of two more killings?
13. In what year was Mikhail Popkov born?
14. What moratorium prevented Mikhail Popkov from facing the death penalty in Russia?
15. What nickname did Russian media give Popkov due to the timing of when his victims' bodies were found?

Daniel Camargo Barbosa

1. What was the birth date of Daniel Camargo Barbosa?
2. How many young girls is Daniel Camargo Barbosa believed to have murdered in Colombia and Ecuador?
3. Who killed Daniel Camargo Barbosa in prison, and what was their relationship to one of his victims?
4. What was the reported IQ of Daniel Camargo Barbosa?
5. Why did Camargo's stepmother dress him as a girl and send him to school like that?
6. In what year was Camargo first arrested, and for what crime?
7. What was the name of Camargo's accomplice in his early crimes?
8. What crime led to Camargo's arrest in 1974 in Barranquilla, Colombia?
9. Where was Camargo imprisoned in Colombia, often referred to as the "Colombian Alcatraz"?
10. How did Camargo escape from Gorgona prison in 1984?
11. In which city and country was Camargo arrested in February 1986, following the murder of a 9-year-old girl named Elizabeth?
12. What book was Camargo carrying when he was arrested in 1986?
13. How many years in prison was Camargo sentenced to in Ecuador in 1989?
14. Who was the notorious serial killer that Camargo was imprisoned with in Ecuador?
15. How old was Camargo when he was killed in prison?

Pedro Rodrigues Filho

1. What was the birthdate of Pedro Rodrigues Filho?
2. What was one of the nicknames given to Pedro Rodrigues Filho?
3. How old was Pedro Rodrigues Filho when he began his vigilante crime spree?
4. What motivated Rodrigues to kill an entire gang?
5. How many murders was Pedro Rodrigues Filho officially sentenced for?
6. In what year was Rodrigues first released from prison after serving 34 years?
7. What crime led to Rodrigues' second prison sentence in 2011?
8. What is the name of Rodrigues' YouTube channel after his second release from prison?
9. Which popular fictional character was inspired by Pedro Rodrigues Filho?
10. How did Pedro Rodrigues Filho die?

Hoshang Amini

1. What nickname did Hoshang Amini earn for his method of disposing of his victims?
2. In which city did Hoshang Amini commit his murders from 1954 to 1962?
3. How many people did Hoshang Amini confess to murdering?
4. Which Iranian serial killer did Amini claim to be inspired by?
5. What type of victims did Amini primarily target for his crimes?
6. How did Amini typically dispose of his victims' bodies?
7. Who was the most prolific known serial killer in Iran's history before Hoshang Amini?
8. What was found in Mesgarabad that brought national attention to Amini's crimes?
9. How did police eventually apprehend Hoshang Amini, according to one version of the story?
10. What was the nickname given to Amini by some newspapers due to his appearance?
11. Which famous Iranian composer recorded interviews with Amini while he was on death row?
12. In which year was Hoshang Amini publicly executed?
13. What did Amini say to two journalists moments before his execution?
14. What book was published in 2015 about Amini's crimes, and who wrote it?

Yang Xinhai

1. What is the birth date of Yang Xinhai?
2. What were the aliases Yang Xinhai was also known by?
3. How many murders and rapes did Yang Xinhai confess to committing between 1999 and 2003?
4. What nickname did the media give to Yang Xinhai?
5. In which year did Yang Xinhai drop out of school?
6. For which crime was Yang sentenced to five years in prison in 1996?
7. Between which years did Yang's killings take place?
8. In which provinces did Yang Xinhai commit his killings?
9. What type of tools did Yang Xinhai typically use to murder his victims?
10. What unusual clothing habit did Yang Xinhai follow during his killings?
11. What happened during an attack in October 2002 that involved a pregnant woman?
12. On what date was Yang Xinhai arrested?
13. On what date was Yang Xinhai sentenced to death?
14. What method of execution was used for Yang Xinhai?
15. According to some media reports, what was the initial motive behind Yang's killings?
16. What later motive was suggested by other media reports for Yang's crimes?
17. What did Yang Xinhai reportedly say about his feelings towards killing and society?

Samuel Little

1. How many murders did Samuel Little confess to committing between 1970 and 2005?
2. What was the name of the FBI program that confirmed Little's involvement in at least 60 murders?
3. Where was Samuel Little born?
4. What occupation did Little claim to have worked at various times in the late 1960s?
5. In which state was Little arrested in 1982 for the murder of Melinda Rose LaPree?
6. What year was Little arrested at a homeless shelter in Louisville, Kentucky?
7. How many life sentences was Little ultimately sentenced to for his crimes?
8. In what year did Little begin confessing to dozens of murders?
9. What method did Samuel Little use to kill most of his victims?
10. What did Little begin doing in exchange for being transferred out of Los Angeles County prison in 2018?
11. In what year did Little die, and where did it happen?
12. How many total murders did the police formally connect Little to?
13. What was the name of Little's long-term girlfriend who supported them both through shoplifting?
14. How many confirmed murders was Little convicted of during his lifetime?

15. In what year did Little receive his first DNA match to a victim's case?

William Unek

1. What was William Unek's profession?
2. How many people did William Unek kill during his two murder sprees?
3. In which country did William Unek commit his first murder spree?
4. Among Unek's victims during his second spree, which two individuals did he reportedly kill by burning?
5. Who was one of Unek's victims that had a personal relationship with him?
6. How long did Unek evade capture after his second murder spree?
7. What reward amount was offered for information leading to Unek's capture?
8. Who played a key role in capturing Unek by engaging him in conversation until help arrived?
9. What type of bomb was used to capture Unek?

Mohammed Bijeh

1. What nationality was serial killer Mohammed Bijeh?
2. How many young boys was Mohammed Bijeh convicted of raping and killing?
3. Between which years did Mohammed Bijeh's crimes take place?
4. What sentence did Mohammed Bijeh receive after being convicted?
5. What was the age range of the boys Bijeh targeted?
6. How did Bijeh describe his motive for committing the murders?
7. At what age did Bijeh move to Khatunabad with his family?
8. What traumatic experiences did Bijeh endure during his childhood?
9. When was Bijeh arrested by the police?
10. What did Bijeh say he would do if he were not arrested?
11. In which town was Bijeh executed in front of a crowd?
12. How many people witnessed Bijeh's public execution?
13. Who managed to stab Bijeh before his execution?
14. How did Bijeh die during his execution?

Andrei Chikatilo

1. What was Andrei Chikatilo's nickname due to the nature and location of his crimes?
2. In which year did Andrei Chikatilo begin his known killing spree?
3. How many murders did Chikatilo confess to?
4. How many murders was Chikatilo ultimately convicted of?
5. What was the method of Andrei Chikatilo's execution?
6. Where was Andrei Chikatilo born?
7. What severe event in Ukraine coincided with Chikatilo's early childhood?
8. Which war greatly impacted Chikatilo's early life?
9. How did Chikatilo's mother explain the disappearance of his older brother, Stepan?
10. What issue did Chikatilo struggle with during his adolescence that worsened his social awkwardness?
11. What position did Chikatilo hold in his school's Communist Party committee at the age of 16?
12. What was Chikatilo's first profession after completing his vocational training?
13. In what city did Chikatilo relocate to in 1961, where he eventually began his teaching career?
14. What were Chikatilo's reported methods of achieving sexual arousal and release during his crimes?
15. What year was Chikatilo first arrested in connection to his crimes, although he was released?

16. How did police eventually connect Chikatilo to his crimes despite discrepancies in blood type testing?

17. What method did Chikatilo frequently use to lure his young victims?

18. What role did Dr. Alexandr Bukhanovsky play in Chikatilo's capture and confession?

19. What superstition did Chikatilo initially believe regarding the eyes of his victims?

20. What Soviet city was the site of Chikatilo's trial?

Anatoly Onoprienko

1. What was Anatoly Onoprienko's nickname?
2. How many people did Anatoly Onoprienko confess to killing?
3. Where was Anatoly Onoprienko born?
4. At what age did Anatoly Onoprienko's mother pass away?
5. Who did Onoprienko claim was responsible for giving him commands to kill?
6. In which year did Onoprienko commit his first murders?
7. How many people were killed during the 1989 family murder that Onoprienko confessed to?
8. What weapon did Onoprienko often use during his murders?
9. Which family did Onoprienko murder on December 24, 1995?
10. In January 1996, how many people did Onoprienko allegedly kill on the Berdyansk–Dnieprovs'k highway?
11. What happened to the Pilat family in January 1996?
12. What method did Onoprienko use to kill the Dubchak family in February 1996?
13. What did Onoprienko usually do to the buildings after killing the occupants?
14. Who was tortured and killed by SBU members during the investigation into the murders?
15. In which year was Onoprienko finally captured?
16. What happened to Onoprienko's death sentence after Ukraine joined the Council of Europe?

17. At what age did Onoprienko die?

Florisvaldo de Oliveira

1. What was Florisvaldo de Oliveira's nickname?
2. In what year was Florisvaldo de Oliveira born?
3. Which state in Brazil was Florisvaldo de Oliveira born in?
4. What was the nickname "Cabo Bruno" based on?
5. During which decade did Cabo Bruno commit most of his murders?
6. How many murders was Cabo Bruno accused of committing?
7. How did José Aparecido Benedito survive his encounter with Cabo Bruno?
8. What type of cars did Cabo Bruno use in his crimes?
9. What year was Cabo Bruno first arrested?
10. How many murders did Cabo Bruno confess to when he was first arrested?
11. What was the length of Cabo Bruno's prison sentence?
12. How many times did Cabo Bruno escape from prison?
13. What was Cabo Bruno's occupation in prison after he became an evangelical?
14. In what year did Cabo Bruno request a change to a semi-open prison regime?
15. What event happened to Cabo Bruno on August 22, 2012?
16. How long did Cabo Bruno spend in prison before being granted freedom?
17. How many times was Cabo Bruno shot when he was killed?
18. Where was Cabo Bruno returning from when he was gunned down?
19. What two types of guns were used in Cabo Bruno's execution?
20. What did Cabo Bruno's family do with his paintings after his death?

Gary Ridgway

1. What is Gary Ridgway commonly known as?
2. How many murders was Ridgway initially convicted of?
3. What type of victims did Ridgway primarily target?
4. How did Ridgway kill most of his victims?
5. In what area were most of Ridgway's victims found?
6. What nickname did the media give Ridgway before his identity was revealed?
7. What technological advancement helped link Ridgway to the murders?
8. In what year was Ridgway arrested?
9. What was Ridgway's occupation when he was arrested?
10. What plea deal did Ridgway agree to in exchange for avoiding the death penalty?
11. What sentence did Ridgway receive?
12. How old was Ridgway when he was born, and where?
13. What unusual behavior did Ridgway display towards his mother during his childhood?
14. What condition did Ridgway struggle with that impacted his schooling?
15. What crime did Ridgway commit at the age of 16?
16. How did Ridgway's first marriage end?
17. What religious behavior did Ridgway exhibit during his second marriage?
18. How many known victims did Ridgway murder after his marriage to Judith Mawson?
19. What advice did Ted Bundy give to investigators about Ridgway's

behavior?

20. When did Ridgway pass a polygraph test related to the murders?

21. How many murders did Ridgway confess to during his plea hearings?

22. In what state did Ridgway dispose of some victims to mislead authorities?

23. What did Ridgway claim reduced his desire to kill after committing necrophilia?

24. How many life sentences was Ridgway given without the possibility of parole?

25. Where is Gary Ridgway currently incarcerated?

Alexander Pichushkin

1. What is Alexander Pichushkin's nickname, based on his connection to chess?
2. How many people is Pichushkin believed to have killed, according to the text?
3. In what year was Pichushkin sentenced to life imprisonment?
4. Where were many of Pichushkin's victims' bodies found?
5. What incident in Pichushkin's childhood is believed to have damaged his frontal cortex?
6. Who recognized Pichushkin's intelligence and encouraged him to pursue chess?
7. What game did Pichushkin excel at, which he learned from his grandfather?
8. What was the name of Pichushkin's first murder victim?
9. What weapon did Pichushkin often use to kill his victims?
10. What did Pichushkin sometimes impale into the skulls of his victims as a signature?
11. What did Pichushkin claim he felt like when deciding if his victims should live or die?
12. Which other Russian serial killer was Pichushkin allegedly competing with?
13. How many squares did Pichushkin aim to match with his killings, according to his early statements?
14. In what location was Pichushkin's final victim, Marina Moskalyova,

murdered?

15. What clue led the authorities to arrest Pichushkin after his final murder?

16. How many murders was Pichushkin convicted of committing?

17. What type of facility was Pichushkin sentenced to for his first 15 years?

18. In which penal colony is Pichushkin currently serving his sentence, as of 2017?

Ahmad Suradji

1. What is Ahmad Suradji also known as?
2. How many girls and women did Ahmad Suradji admit to killing?
3. Between which years did Ahmad Suradji commit his murders?
4. How did Ahmad Suradji kill his victims?
5. In what type of field did Ahmad Suradji bury his victims?
6. What city did Ahmad Suradji live in?
7. What occupation did Ahmad Suradji have in addition to being a serial killer?
8. What did Ahmad Suradji claim his father told him to do in a dream?
9. Why did Ahmad Suradji decide to kill instead of waiting for women to die naturally?
10. Who was one of Suradji's victims who led to his arrest?
11. How many bodies were exhumed from the sugarcane field where Suradji buried his victims?
12. What did Ahmad Suradji drink from his victims to gain "mystical" powers?
13. Who assisted Ahmad Suradji in committing the murders?
14. When did Ahmad Suradji's trial begin?
15. What was the outcome of Ahmad Suradji's trial?
16. How was Ahmad Suradji executed, and on what date?

Raman Raghav

1. What were some of the aliases used by Raman Raghav?
2. During what period was Raman Raghav active as a serial killer?
3. How many people were attacked in the first round of murders committed by Raman Raghav in 1965-1966?
4. What object did Raghav use to commit his murders?
5. Which police officer recognized and arrested Raman Raghav in 1968?
6. How many murders did Raghav confess to committing in 1966?
7. What mental condition did a psychiatrist from Nair Hospital claim Raghav suffered from during his trial?
8. What was Raghav's final sentence after his trial?
9. In which hospital did Raman Raghav die in 1995?
10. How did Raman Raghav's sentence change in 1987?

Moses Sithole

1. What nickname was given to Moses Sithole's series of murders?
2. How many women and toddlers did Moses Sithole murder between July 1994 and November 1995?
3. Where is Moses Sithole currently incarcerated?
4. What significant life event occurred when Sithole was five years old?
5. How long was Moses Sithole imprisoned in his teens for rape?
6. What organization was Sithole managing at the time of his crimes?
7. What method did Sithole typically use to kill his victims?
8. Who visited Boksburg in person to appeal for help in capturing Sithole?
9. In which year was Moses Sithole sentenced for his crimes?
10. What was the total number of years Sithole was sentenced to in prison?
11. At what age would Moses Sithole become eligible for parole?
12. What two diseases did Sithole test positive for after his capture?

Gennady Mikhasevich

1. What was Gennady Mikhasevich's nationality?
2. How many women did Gennady Mikhasevich murder?
3. In what year did Mikhasevich commit his first murder?
4. What event in Mikhasevich's personal life led to his first killing spree?
5. How did Mikhasevich typically kill his victims?
6. What type of car did Mikhasevich use to lure his victims in his later murders?
7. What organization did Mikhasevich pretend to be part of in his attempt to derail the investigation?
8. How many handwriting samples did the investigators analyze before discovering Mikhasevich's resemblance to the murderer's notes?
9. What year was Mikhasevich finally arrested?
10. What was Mikhasevich's final sentence and how was it carried out?

Vera Renczi

1. What nickname was Vera Renczi given?
2. How many individuals did Vera Renczi allegedly poison?
3. What substance did Renczi use to poison her victims?
4. Who was Vera Renczi's first husband, and what was his profession?
5. What did Vera Renczi claim had happened to her first husband after poisoning him?
6. How old was Vera Renczi when she moved to Nagybecskerek with her father?
7. According to sources, what personality trait did Vera Renczi exhibit during her teenage years?
8. What significant event in Vera Renczi's early life led to her becoming "unmanageable" by the age of fifteen?
9. How did the police finally discover Renczi's cellar containing coffins?
10. How many coffins were discovered in the underground cellar?
11. What did Vera Renczi claim was her motivation for killing her victims?
12. What did Vera Renczi confess about her habit of sitting in the underground cellar?
13. Why was Vera Renczi not executed despite being sentenced to death?
14. In what year did Vera Renczi die?
15. Which criminal case, not Vera Renczi's, inspired the play "Arsenic and Old Lace"?
16. In which TV series was Vera Renczi featured in a reenactment of her story?

Fernando Hernández Leyva

1. In what year was Fernando Hernández Leyva born?
2. How many murders was Fernando Hernández Leyva convicted of in 1986?
3. How many murders did Leyva confess to?
4. What is the suspected number of actual murders committed by Leyva?
5. Over how many years did Leyva's criminal activity take place?
6. How many times did Leyva escape from prison before his final capture?
7. In what year was Leyva arrested for the final time?
8. What was Leyva's attempted method of suicide in prison?
9. Why did Leyva's suicide attempt fail?
10. After his final arrest, how many states in Mexico were his crimes confirmed to have taken place in?
11. What nickname was Fernando Hernández Leyva known by?
12. During his trial, what did Leyva claim was the reason for his confessions?
13. Which authorities did not comment on Leyva's retraction of his confessions during his trial?
14. In which Mexican state is the "La Palma" prison where Leyva is currently being held?
15. In what year would Leyva potentially be released from prison if he completes his sentence?

John Wayne Gacy

1. What was John Wayne Gacy's nickname due to his performances as a clown?
2. How many known victims did John Wayne Gacy murder?
3. Where did Gacy bury most of his victims?
4. In which year was Gacy first convicted of sodomy?
5. What led to John Wayne Gacy's arrest in 1978?
6. How was Gacy typically killing his victims?
7. What was Gacy's final meal before his execution?
8. Which U.S. state did Gacy commit his murders in?
9. What condition did Gacy have as a child that caused him to avoid sports?
10. How many years was Gacy on death row before his execution?
11. What led to Gacy being referred to as the "Killer Clown"?
12. In what year was Gacy executed?
13. What was the relationship between Gacy and his father?
14. How did Gacy lure many of his victims to his home?
15. Which investigation ultimately led to Gacy's arrest?
16. What method of execution was used for Gacy?
17. What profession did Gacy claim as part of his community involvement that hid his crimes for so long?
18. What mental disorder did Gacy's defense team claim he had during his trial?
19. How did Gacy dispose of some victims when he ran out of space in his crawl space?

20. What was discovered during the first search of Gacy's house that raised suspicions?

Ali Asghar Borujerdi

1. What was Ali Asghar Borujerdi's more infamous nickname?
2. In which two countries did Asghar commit his murders?
3. How many people did Asghar confess to killing in total?
4. What age was Asghar when he was first arrested for his crimes?
5. What type of people were typically Asghar's victims?
6. What relation did Asghar's father and grandfather have to crime?
7. In which city did Asghar murder 25 children and adolescents before fleeing to Iran?
8. After returning to Iran, in which city did Asghar settle and continue his crimes?
9. How did the authorities first become suspicious of Asghar when they encountered him in Tehran?
10. What was the fate of Asghar after his trial and conviction?
11. How many murders was Asghar convicted of committing in Iran?
12. What reason did Asghar give for killing the boys he targeted?

Vasili Komaroff

1. What was Vasili Ivanovich Komaroff's birth name?
2. How many people was Komaroff convicted of killing in Moscow?
3. What was Komaroff's profession when he committed the murders?
4. In which year did Komaroff begin his series of murders?
5. What method did Komaroff typically use to kill his victims?
6. How did Komaroff dispose of most of the bodies?
7. Who eventually joined Komaroff in committing the murders?
8. How did the police eventually discover Komaroff's crimes?
9. How many times did Komaroff attempt to commit suicide while in prison?
10. What year were Komaroff and his wife executed?
11. What did Komaroff describe killing as during his interview?
12. In which street did Komaroff and his family live when the murders took place?
13. What triggered the initial police visit to Komaroff's home?
14. What was Komaroff's motive for the murders?
15. How many of Komaroff's victims' bodies were ultimately recovered by police?
16. What was the result of Komaroff's forensic psychiatric examination?

Radik Tagirov

1. What is the nickname given to Radik Tagirov?
2. In which region did Radik Tagirov commit his murders?
3. What profession did Tagirov pursue before becoming a vagrant?
4. How many elderly women did Tagirov murder between 2011 and 2012?
5. What age range did Tagirov's victims fall into?
6. How did Tagirov typically gain access to his victims' homes?
7. What method did Tagirov use to kill his victims?
8. In which city were the first nine murders committed?
9. What significant piece of evidence was captured on CCTV in September 2012?
10. What was the reward offered in 2013 for information on the case?
11. What year was a Kazakh native arrested on suspicion of being involved in the murders?
12. What type of evidence was crucial in identifying Tagirov as the killer?
13. How many murders did Tagirov confess to after being detained?
14. When did Tagirov's trial begin?
15. What was the final sentence given to Radik Tagirov in March 2024?

Karl Denke

1. What nickname was Karl Denke given due to his actions as a serial killer and cannibal?
2. In what year did Karl Denke begin his series of murders?
3. What profession did Denke attempt before turning to crime, which ultimately failed?
4. What items did Denke sell in his shop that were suspected to contain human remains?
5. What role did Denke volunteer for at his local Lutheran church before quitting his membership in 1906?
6. Who was Karl Denke's first known victim?
7. What happened to the slaughterhouse worker, Eduard Trautmann, in relation to one of Denke's victims, Emma Sander?
8. What did Denke do with the flesh of his victims that shocked the public?
9. Who was Denke's last known victim?
10. What led to Karl Denke's arrest in December 1924?
11. How did Karl Denke die before he could be interrogated by authorities?
12. What disturbing items were found in Denke's home during the police search?
13. How many victims were confirmed in Denke's ledger?
14. What is the estimated number of Karl Denke's total victims based on the body parts found?
15. What remains unknown about Karl Denke's life and crimes, despite the discovery of his murders?

Monster of the Mangones

1. What nickname was given to the unidentified Colombian serial killer who murdered young boys in Cali during the 1960s and 1970s?
2. How many victims is the Monster of the Mangones believed to have killed?
3. What was the modus operandi of the Monster of the Mangones?
4. Which syndrome is the Monster of the Mangones speculated to have suffered from?
5. In what year was the body of the first victim, a paperboy, discovered?
6. What significant feature was missing from the third victim found near the Aguacatal River?
7. How did the authorities initially explain the discovery of the murdered boys' bodies?
8. Between which months in 1964 did the Monster of the Mangones' crimes temporarily cease?
9. What is the estimated total number of young boys and men killed by the Monster of the Mangones?
10. What is the name of the film inspired by the Monster of the Mangones case, and who directed it?
11. What condition does the character in the film *Pura sangre* suffer from that requires him to drink blood?

Milton Sipalo

1. Who was Milton Mufungulwa Sipalo also known as?
2. How many women and girls did Sipalo murder between January and September 1980?
3. How was Sipalo arrested on 16 September 1980?
4. What was Sipalo's modus operandi in committing his crimes?
5. What unusual detail was often found on Sipalo's victims' bodies?
6. Who were the typical victims of Sipalo, in terms of ethnicity or language?
7. What was the name of the operation launched by the police to capture Sipalo?
8. What methods did the police use to try to capture Sipalo during "Operation Rosemary"?
9. How did the police attempt to lure Sipalo by using undercover detectives?
10. What did Sipalo's first surviving victim manage to do during her attack to escape?
11. What led the police to suspect that the perpetrator was a soldier or someone impersonating one?
12. What happened to the Petauke woman who was approached by soldiers along with the second surviving victim?
13. How did the second surviving victim recognize Sipalo at the bus station?
14. What was found at Sipalo's home when the police searched it?
15. How did Sipalo respond when confronted with the fact that the survivors had identified him as their attacker?
16. What did Sipalo do on 18 September 1980 that led to his death?

Zhang Jun

1. In which year was Zhang Jun born?
2. How many stores did Zhang Jun and his associates rob between June 1993 and September 2000?
3. How many people were killed by Zhang Jun and his associates during their robberies?
4. What was the total amount of money stolen by Zhang Jun and his associates?
5. Why did Zhang Jun drop out of high school?
6. What crime was Zhang Jun arrested for in 1989?
7. How much gold jewelry did Zhang Jun steal during the robbery of the Chongqing Friendship store in 1995?
8. On what date did Zhang Jun rob Shanghai's first department store?
9. During the Changsha Friendship Mall robbery in 1997, how many people were killed, and what was the value of the gold jewelry stolen?
10. How many people were killed when Zhang Jun raided a public security checkpoint and toll station in Hebei Province in 1998?
11. How much gold jewelry did Zhang Jun steal during the robbery at Wuhan Square in 1999?
12. What was Zhang Jun's target when he robbed the Agricultural Bank of Anxiang County in 2000?
13. How many people were killed during the robbery of a cash truck in Changde on September 1, 2000?
14. What happened during Zhang Jun's 1993 robbery attempt in Anxiang

County?

15. How did Zhang Jun avoid capture after accidentally injuring his companion in the failed robbery of 1993?

16. What weapon did Zhang Jun allegedly have with him at the time of his arrest?

17. Who personally interrogated Zhang Jun after his arrest?

18. When was Zhang Jun sentenced to death?

19. On what date was Zhang Jun executed?

Mariam Soulakiotis

1. What was Abbess Mariam Soulakiotis' birth name?
2. What was the nickname given to Mariam Soulakiotis by contemporary media?
3. How many years in total was Mariam Soulakiotis sentenced to after her trials?
4. What was the name of the monastery founded by Mariam Soulakiotis and Archbishop Matthew?
5. In what year was Mariam Soulakiotis arrested?
6. What was the main method Mariam Soulakiotis used to gain wealth for the monastery, according to allegations?
7. How many negligent homicides was Mariam Soulakiotis accused of due to her tuberculosis treatment practices?
8. Which organization traced a missing woman, Simela Spyrides, to Mariam Soulakiotis' monastery?
9. How did Mariam Soulakiotis die, and where?
10. What is the commonly cited figure for the total number of Mariam Soulakiotis' victims, including both murders and negligent homicides?
11. What was the justification Mariam Soulakiotis' defense attorney gave for the property being in her name?
12. Which war did Field Marshal Harold Alexander allegedly thank Mariam Soulakiotis' monastery for helping British soldiers escape from?
13. Where is the Panagia Pefkovounogiatrissa Monastery located?
14. What religious figure did Mariam Soulakiotis' followers venerate even

after her death?

15. Which sect of Greek Orthodoxy did Mariam Soulakiotis follow, considered schismatic by mainstream and other Old Calendarist groups?

16. How many police officers participated in the raid on Mariam Soulakiotis' monastery in December 1950?

17. What term was used to describe Mariam Soulakiotis by modern secular historians?

18. Where is Mariam Soulakiotis buried?

Cedric Maake

1. What was Maoupa Cedric Maake's occupation before he started committing crimes?
2. In what South African city did Maake live when he began his life of crime?
3. What year did Maake start committing his murders?
4. Why was Maake referred to as the "Wemmer Pan Killer"?
5. What types of weapons did Maake often use in his attacks?
6. How many murder victims was Maake convicted of killing?
7. How did the South African police initially profile Maake's crimes?
8. What technology did the police use to aid in the prosecution of Maake?
9. What alias did Maake use when selling a bicycle belonging to one of his victims?
10. How many life sentences was Maake sentenced to?
11. How many total charges was Maake convicted of?
12. How many years in prison was Maake sentenced to overall?

Robert Pickton

1. What was Robert Pickton's profession before he became known as a serial killer?
2. In what time period did Robert Pickton commit most of his murders?
3. How many murders did Robert Pickton confess to?
4. How many murders was Pickton convicted of in 2007?
5. What was the sentence given to Robert Pickton after his conviction?
6. What significant issue did the discovery of Pickton's crimes highlight in Canada?
7. What inquiry was formed as a result of the investigation into Pickton's crimes?
8. What was the name of the farm owned by the Pickton brothers?
9. What nickname was given to the ad hoc nightclub Pickton operated on his farm?
10. Who was the sex worker that survived an attack by Pickton in 1997?
11. What was the name of the brother who co-owned the farm with Robert Pickton?
12. What happened to the remaining 20 murder charges against Pickton after his initial trial?
13. What was one of the disturbing claims made about how Pickton disposed of his victims?
14. How many counts of second-degree murder was Pickton found guilty of in 2007?
15. Which two items found on Pickton's farm linked him to the murders of

Andrea Borhaven and Cara Ellis?

16. In what year did the Missing Women Commission of Inquiry release its final report?

17. What fictional crime drama alluded to Pickton's crimes in its storyline?

18. What biographical horror film about Pickton was released in 2023?

19. What controversial item of clothing caused outrage in 2024, linked to Pickton's crimes?

Bruce George Peter Lee

1. What is the birth name of Peter Tredget?
2. How many counts of manslaughter did Tredget plead guilty to?
3. What significant event occurred on December 4, 1979, involving Tredget?
4. How did Charles Hastie manage to escape during the fire at Selby Street?
5. What was the relationship between Peter Tredget and Charles Hastie?
6. How many fires did Tredget confess to starting, including the one at Selby Street?
7. What were the outcomes of the public inquiry regarding the Wensley Lodge fire?
8. Which hospital was Tredget initially taken to after his conviction?
9. In what year did Tredget change his name from Bruce George Peter Lee?
10. What significant legal action did Detective Superintendent Ron Sagar take against The Sunday Times?

The Stoneman

1. How many murders were attributed to the Stoneman in Calcutta during 1989?
2. In which two cities did the Stoneman murders take place between 1983 and 1989?
3. What was the method of killing used by the Stoneman?
4. What key fact remains unresolved about the Stoneman murders in Calcutta and Mumbai?
5. Which police force noticed a pattern after the sixth murder in the Mumbai killings?
6. How did the only known survivor of the Stoneman attack in Mumbai describe the attacker?
7. What stopped the killings in Mumbai in 1988, according to the text?
8. What happened after a series of arrests in Calcutta in connection with the Stoneman murders?
9. In what year and city were similar incidents to the Stoneman murders reported after 1989?
10. What film, released in 2009, was based on the Stoneman murders?
11. How much of the 2009 film *The Stoneman Murders* was said to be based on fact, according to the writer-director?
12. Which Bengali film released in 2011 depicted a plot inspired by the Stoneman murders in Calcutta?

Juan Corona

1. In which U.S. state did Juan Corona commit his crimes?
2. How many murders was Juan Corona convicted of in 1973?
3. What was discovered in the peach orchards along the Feather River in 1971?
4. What type of therapy did Juan Corona receive in 1956 after being diagnosed with schizophrenia?
5. What evidence linked Juan Corona to the murders of the farm workers?
6. How many victims were identified in total by June 4, 1971?
7. Who replaced Corona's first legal defender, Roy Van den Heuvel, in 1971?
8. How many counts of first-degree murder was Corona charged with in his first trial?
9. What was the outcome of Corona's second trial in 1982?
10. What did the jury find most incriminating in Corona's second trial?

Fritz Haarmann

1. What were the three infamous nicknames given to Fritz Haarmann due to his crimes?
2. In which city did Fritz Haarmann commit his murders?
3. How many murders was Haarmann found guilty of, out of the total number he was tried for?
4. What method did Haarmann commonly use to kill his victims?
5. What was Haarmann's childhood like in terms of his behavior and interests?
6. What happened to Haarmann after he was diagnosed with "equivalent to epilepsy" during his military service?
7. How did Haarmann manage to escape from the mental institution in 1898?
8. What occupation did Haarmann briefly attempt after being discharged from the military?
9. Who was Haarmann's criminal accomplice and lover?
10. What was the name of Haarmann's first known victim?
11. Where did Haarmann dispose of many of his victims' dismembered remains?
12. What rumors circulated about Haarmann selling his victims' flesh?
13. How did Haarmann get involved with the police as an informant?
14. What major event occurred in Germany following World War I, contributing to increased crime rates?
15. What was Haarmann's "love bite"?

16. What role did Hans Grans play in Haarmann's crimes, according to some testimonies?
17. Where were the remains of Haarmann's victims buried?
18. What was the cause of Haarmann's execution in 1925?
19. How many victims did Haarmann confess to murdering, according to his own estimate during interrogation?
20. How did Haarmann explain his urge to murder his victims during his trial?
21. What happened to Haarmann's brain after his execution?
22. What was a major social issue that arose in Germany following Haarmann's crimes?
23. Who was Haarmann's executioner?
24. What year was the memorial for Haarmann's victims erected in Stöckener Cemetery?

Béla Kiss

1. What was Béla Kiss' profession?
2. How many bodies were found in the barrels on Béla Kiss' property?
3. What event led to the discovery of the bodies in Béla Kiss' barrels?
4. What did Béla Kiss claim he was storing in the metal drums when questioned by the police?
5. During World War I, what happened to Béla Kiss, prompting his landlord to visit his property?
6. What items were found in Béla Kiss' secret room?
7. What was discovered about Béla Kiss' victims in terms of their personal circumstances?
8. What did the puncture marks on the bodies suggest Béla Kiss might have been practicing?
9. What happened when the authorities attempted to arrest Béla Kiss in 1916?
10. What false identity was Béla Kiss thought to have used during his escape?
11. What was the last reported sighting of Béla Kiss, and where did it take place?

Yvan Keller

1. When and where was Yvan Keller born?
2. What was Yvan Keller's nickname as a serial killer?
3. How many people did Yvan Keller confess to killing?
4. What was the occupation of Yvan Keller's father?
5. At what age was Yvan Keller first arrested, and for what crime?
6. After his release from prison, what kind of business did Yvan Keller start?
7. What was the name of Keller's first companion, whom he allegedly forced into prostitution?
8. What did Yvan Keller do when he found out his second wife, Séverine, was in a relationship with another man?
9. What was the common method Yvan Keller used to kill his victims?
10. How many times was Yvan Keller denounced to authorities before his final arrest?
11. How did Yvan Keller die, and where did it happen?

Ronald Dominique

1. What is Ronald Dominique's nickname as a serial killer?
2. How many people did Ronald Dominique murder?
3. What was Ronald Dominique's birth date?
4. In which state did Ronald Dominique commit his murders?
5. What was the span of years during which Dominique's murders occurred?
6. When was Dominique convicted and sentenced to life imprisonment?
7. Which organization described Dominique's case as the most significant serial homicide case in the last two decades?
8. What was the profession of Dominique's parents?
9. What type of lifestyle did Dominique lead after dropping out of college?
10. What charge was Dominique first arrested for in 1985?
11. Why was Dominique's case in 1996 dismissed?
12. What role did Dominique often take in the local gay community?
13. How did Dominique lure his victims?
14. Who was Dominique's first confirmed victim?
15. How was Dominique's first confirmed victim, David Mitchell, originally believed to have died?
16. What was Dominique's common method of killing his victims?
17. In which parish did Dominique's first murders take place?
18. Who was Dominique's last confirmed victim?
19. How did Dominique come under police suspicion?
20. Where was Dominique living when he was arrested?
21. How many murders did Dominique confess to?

22. What was Dominique's stated reason for killing his victims?
23. How did Dominique avoid the death penalty?
24. Where is Dominique currently incarcerated?

94

Juan Fernando Hermosa

1. In what year was Juan Fernando Hermosa Suárez born?
2. What nickname was Juan Fernando Hermosa Suárez given due to his crimes?
3. At what age did Hermosa begin leading a gang of youngsters?
4. How many murders did Hermosa commit in total?
5. What weapon did Hermosa use to commit his murders?
6. What group was put in charge of investigating Hermosa's crimes?
7. During which incident did Hermosa's mother die?
8. How old was Hermosa when he was captured by the police?
9. What was the maximum prison sentence Hermosa received as a minor?
10. What did Hermosa manage to obtain through his girlfriend while in prison?
11. How did Hermosa escape from prison in 1993?
12. What happened to Hermosa on his 20th birthday?

Earle Nelson

1. What was Earle Nelson's nickname in the media during his crime spree?
2. In which two cities did Nelson begin his killing spree in 1926?
3. What was Nelson's modus operandi when targeting his victims?
4. How did Nelson kill most of his victims?
5. Who was Nelson's penultimate victim, and what was unique about her murder compared to his other victims?
6. How many murders and other attacks is Nelson believed to have committed, according to recent research?
7. What was the cause of death of Nelson's parents, Frances Nelson and James Carlos Ferral?
8. At what age was Nelson expelled from school, and what incident occurred when he was 10 years old that affected his behavior?
9. Where was Nelson first institutionalized after exhibiting bizarre behavior in adulthood?
10. What year was Nelson arrested for the final time, and in which country was he executed?
11. Which 1943 film by Alfred Hitchcock was inspired by Nelson's crimes?
12. What unusual religious behavior did Nelson exhibit as a child and throughout his life?
13. What was the verdict and punishment given to Nelson after his trial in Winnipeg?
14. Which passage from the Bible did Nelson obsess over during his incarceration?

15. What were Nelson's last words before his execution?

Patrick Kearney

1. What was Patrick Wayne Kearney's nickname?
2. How many young men and boys did Kearney murder?
3. What was Kearney's occupation?
4. In what year did Kearney commit his first murder?
5. What was the name of the victim whose body was buried behind Kearney's garage?
6. Which year did Kearney begin committing murders on a near-monthly basis?
7. How did Kearney typically kill his victims?
8. What was the name of Kearney's youngest known victim?
9. Who was the victim that led to Kearney's arrest?
10. How many murders did Kearney initially confess to?
11. What type of sentence did Kearney receive for his crimes?

William Bonin

1. What nickname was William Bonin known by due to where his victims were found?
2. How many murders was Bonin convicted of, and how many did he confess to?
3. Who was Bonin's first known murder victim?
4. What method did Bonin typically use to kill his victims?
5. What was the role of Vernon Butts in Bonin's crimes?
6. Where was Bonin executed, and what method was used?
7. What was Bonin's IQ according to psychiatric evaluations?
8. What traumatic experience did Bonin claim happened to him during his childhood at the Franco-American School?
9. Which family member did Bonin have an unhealthy relationship with, contributing to his psychological issues?
10. What did Bonin's wartime experiences reportedly contribute to his criminal behavior?
11. How did Bonin manipulate his psychiatric evaluations during his time in Atascadero State Hospital?
12. What kind of van did Bonin use to abduct his victims, and how did he modify it?
13. What event led to the police starting a surveillance operation on Bonin in June 1980?
14. Who was Bonin's final murder victim, and who helped him commit this murder?

15. How long did Bonin spend on death row before his execution?

16. What did Bonin state was his major life regret during his final interview?

17. What was the nickname of another serial killer, Randy Kraft, who was a friend of Bonin on death row?

18. How did Bonin express his feelings about the death penalty in his final statement?

19. Who was one of Bonin's victims that a coroner theorized had been impaled by a large object?

20. What did Bonin's defense attorneys argue contributed significantly to his criminal behavior during his trials?

III

Answer Key

Luis Garavito

1. La Bestia (The Beast)
2. Colombia
3. 193 victims
4. 1999
5. 1,853 years and 9 days
6. 40 years
7. Severe eye cancer and astigmatism
8. Antisocial personality disorder and narcissistic personality traits
9. Ecuador
10. Catholic priest, schoolteacher
11. A blue notebook
12. Brandy
13. His glasses
14. 2023, age 66
15. Guillermo Prieto "Pirry" La Rotta

Enriqueta Martí

1. 1868
2. "The Vampire of carrer Ponent" or "The Vampire of Barcelona"
3. Teresita Guitart Congost
4. Barcelona
5. Affluent clients with unusual desires, including for children
6. Drinking the blood of children
7. She used their remains to make remedies
8. Tragic Week
9. Claudia Elías
10. Two girls (Teresita and Angelita), a boning knife, bloody clothing, small human bones, and preserved human remains
11. Pepito
12. She claimed he had gone to the country because he was ill
13. From her sister-in-law, claiming Angelita was stillborn
14. She was lynched by her prison mates
15. Uterine cancer
16. They were from animals, not children
17. She was a scapegoat for covering up sexual scandals involving minors from the upper class

Boston Strangler

1. Albert DeSalvo
2. 13 women
3. "The Mad Strangler of Boston"
4. F. Lee Bailey
5. Massachusetts Attorney General Edward W. Brooke
6. He allowed a parapsychologist, Peter Hurkos, to use extrasensory perception to analyze the case.
7. "The Green Man" and "The Measuring Man"
8. 1967
9. He was caught the next day and transferred to a maximum-security prison.
10. Mary Sullivan
11. DNA evidence
12. He believed DeSalvo was not the Boston Strangler.
13. He argued that it was behaviorally impossible for all the murders to be committed by one person.
14. Attorney Elaine Sharp
15. He noted that DeSalvo got the time of death wrong, and there were inconsistencies in the confession.

Peter Sutcliffe

1. The Yorkshire Ripper
2. Thirteen
3. January 1981
4. The voice of God
5. Wilma Mary McCann
6. Manchester
7. Paranoid schizophrenia
8. Lawrence Byford (Byford Report)
9. Nine times
10. 2016
11. Jayne MacDonald
12. A hammer
13. Wearside Jack
14. Failing to catch Sutcliffe despite interviewing him nine times
15. HGV (Heavy Goods Vehicle) driver

Arthur Shawcross

1. The Genesee River Killer
2. Watertown, New York
3. 14 years of a 25-year sentence
4. Food service worker
5. 63 years old, Sullivan Correctional Facility
6. Dr. Michael H. Stone
7. United States Army, 4th Infantry Division
8. One tour of duty
9. His habit of setting fires for sexual arousal
10. Arson and burglary
11. He pleaded guilty to manslaughter due to a lack of direct evidence in one case
12. 14 years
13. Brain damage, multiple personality disorder, post-traumatic stress disorder
14. FBI criminal profiler Robert K. Ressler; he concluded Shawcross's claims were untrue
15. A cyst pressing on his temporal lobe and scarring on his frontal lobes
16. 2003, three victims

Belle Gunness

1. Brynhild Paulsdatter Størseth
2. Illinois and Indiana
3. At least 14 people
4. In a fire, although her fate is unconfirmed
5. Domestic servant and butcher shop worker
6. Mads Ditlev Anton Sørensen
7. Both burned down, resulting in insurance payouts
8. He died of cerebral hemorrhage
9. She bought a pig farm in La Porte, Indiana
10. She claimed a meat grinder fell on his head
11. 1905
12. The fire at her farmhouse, which led to the discovery of multiple graves
13. At least 11 additional bodies were found
14. He was her hired hand and on-and-off lover
15. That Gunness murdered and robbed men who responded to her ads, and he burned down the house at her request
16. The body was five inches shorter and fifty pounds lighter than Belle Gunness
17. The DNA sample could not be properly tested
18. *Method* (2004)
19. *In the Garden of Spite*
20. *My Men* by Victoria Kielland

Carl Eugene Watts

1. Coral
2. Sunday Morning Slasher
3. 13 murders
4. 40 women, implying over 80 victims
5. Killeen, Texas
6. Meningitis
7. By age 12
8. 15 years old
9. Antisocial personality disorder
10. 1973
11. Boxing
12. Zenaida Tomes
13. Sunday Morning Slasher
14. Houston
15. 1982
16. 2004
17. He was convicted and sentenced to life imprisonment
18. Prostate cancer

Monster of Florence

1. 1968 to 1985
2. 16 victims
3. A .22 caliber Beretta handgun
4. Portions of skin surrounding sex organs were excised from female victims
5. Antonio Lo Bianco and Barbara Locci
6. "Queen Bee" (Ape Regina)
7. The discovery that the same gun was used in multiple murders
8. Her corpse was violated with a grapevine stalk and had 97 stab wounds
9. He spoke about the murders before the bodies had been discovered
10. Wilhelm Friedrich Horst Meyer and Jens Uwe Rüsch
11. Police suspected the murders were linked to rituals involving genitalia
12. To "talk to her about her daughter" (Cambi)
13. An unfired bullet of the same brand as the Monster's
14. Mario Vanni and Giancarlo Lotti
15. He claimed the murders were acts of anger due to sexual rejection
16. It was a line of investigation that focused on Sardinian suspects connected to Locci's murder
17. He was a doctor found dead in suspicious circumstances; his death certificate indicated drowning, but later evidence suggested strangulation
18. He was arrested after investigating a favored suspect, later freed, and claimed the Monster case was mishandled
19. Francesco Amicone's investigation

20. Giuseppe Bevilacqua

Lee Choon-jae

1. A South Korean serial killer known for committing the Hwaseong serial murders.
2. Gyeonggi Province.
3. Fifteen.
4. The Hwaseong serial murders.
5. The statute of limitations had expired.
6. The drowning of his younger brother.
7. In 1983, as a tank driver.
8. Breaking into a house in Suwon.
9. Ten.
10. 2 million.
11. The killer was thought to have blood type B, but it was later corrected to type O.
12. Yoon Sung-yeo.
13. They wore red clothes to try to lure the killer.
14. Through DNA evidence from one of the victims' underwear.
15. For the rape and murder of his sister-in-law.
16. More than 30.
17. He didn't want to face public condemnation.
18. It sparked renewed interest in the case.
19. DNA from the underwear of one of the victims matched his.
20. That Yoon was coerced through torture to give a false confession.

Maurizio Minghella

1. Turin
2. Four
3. Five
4. "Travolta of Val Polcevera"
5. The death of his brother in a car crash
6. 70
7. 1977
8. Anna Pagano
9. By writing "Bricato Rose" instead of "Brigate Rosse" on the body
10. A pair of his glasses found at the crime scene
11. Maria Strambelli and Wanda Scerra
12. 1981
13. Carpenter
14. A scarf
15. DNA traces, phone location, and cell phones with deleted numbers
16. Through a laundry and by escaping a hospital
17. 2003
18. Pavia prison

Pedro López

1. The Monster of the Andes
2. Colombia
3. 12 siblings (he was the seventh of 13 children)
4. He was murdered during La Violencia
5. His mother caught him attempting to molest his sister
6. At age 8
7. 1969
8. He killed them after being raped by them
9. Peru
10. The discovery of remains after flash flooding in Ambato, Ecuador
11. Local merchants
12. He used a trinket to lure them
13. 110 confirmed victims
14. 16 years
15. In 1994, for "good behavior"
16. Colombia
17. 1998
18. September 1999
19. 2005
20. Interpol

Ted Bundy

1. Theodore Robert Cowell.
2. By simulating a physical impairment or pretending to be an authority figure.
3. He revisited their bodies, grooming them and performing sex acts until decomposition prevented further interaction.
4. 1975.
5. Three.
6. Ann Rule.
7. He described himself as "the most cold-hearted son of a bitch you'll ever meet."
8. Burlington, Vermont.
9. His maternal grandparents.
10. Bundy stood by her bed smiling, surrounded by kitchen knives.
11. Neighbors reported that Bundy engaged in acts of animal cruelty, such as setting a cat on fire.
12. Downhill skiing.
13. University of Washington.
14. Ann Rule.
15. Diane Edwards.
16. Bundy abruptly stopped contacting Edwards and ignored her calls.
17. Bludgeoning his victims and sexually assaulting them.
18. Janice Ann Ott and Denise Marie Naslund.
19. A Volkswagen Beetle.

20. He jumped from a second-story window and evaded capture for six days.
21. He bludgeoned and strangled two women and severely injured two others.
22. Kimberly Leach.
23. Electric chair.
24. He confessed to necrophilia and revisiting their bodies.
25. He used subtle changes in facial hair and hairstyle.

Chester Turner

1. Chester Dewayne Turner was convicted of sexually assaulting and murdering 14 women and an unborn baby.
2. "The Southside Slayer."
3. 2007.
4. Diane Johnson, found on March 9, 1987.
5. A four-block-wide corridor on either side of Figueroa Street in Los Angeles.
6. Regina Nadine Washington.
7. David Allen Jones, who spent 11 years in prison.
8. Through DNA analysis while he was incarcerated for another crime.
9. In 2014, Turner was convicted of four additional murders and sentenced to death again.
10. The California Supreme Court reversed Turner's conviction for the murder of the unborn baby, but the death sentence for the other 14 victims was upheld.
11. San Quentin State Prison.

Jack the Ripper

1. Whitechapel
2. Whitechapel Murderer, Leather Apron
3. Anatomical or surgical knowledge
4. From the "Dear Boss letter"
5. The "From Hell letter"
6. Mary Ann Nichols, Annie Chapman, Elizabeth Stride, Catherine Eddowes, Mary Jane Kelly
7. 1888
8. Bloody Sunday (1887)
9. Mary Ann Nichols
10. The heart
11. Elizabeth Long
12. Elizabeth Stride and Catherine Eddowes
13. "The Juwes are The men That Will not be Blamed for nothing."
14. Mary Jane Kelly
15. Approximately 80,000
16. It came with half a human kidney
17. £50
18. Ripperology
19. Butcher or slaughterer
20. Frances Coles

Donald Henry Gaskins

1. Donald Henry Parrott Jr.
2. Thirteen people
3. A criminal associate named Walter Neeley led them to the site.
4. Dennis Bellamy
5. Central Correctional Institution (CCI)
6. Using a C4 explosive disguised as a speaker
7. 100 to 110 murders
8. The confession of Walter Neeley
9. His niece, Janice Kirby, and her friend Patricia Ann Alsbrook
10. Gaskins was angry that Doreen had become pregnant with a biracial child.
11. Suzanne Kipper Owens, $1,500
12. "Meanest Man in America"
13. By poisoning his food and drink
14. "I'll let my lawyers talk for me. I'm ready to go."

Charles Ray Hatcher

1. Mound City, Missouri
2. 16 people
3. His oldest brother, Arthur Allen, was electrocuted.
4. Auto theft
5. Six times
6. Steven Pellham
7. The murder of Jerry Tharrington
8. William Freeman
9. Albert Ralph Price
10. Faked mental illness
11. 1971
12. Paranoid schizophrenia
13. December 25, 1978
14. Sexual assault of a 16-year-old boy
15. Melvin Reynolds
16. Michelle Steele
17. 1982
18. He hanged himself in his cell.

Jeffrey Dahmer

1. The Milwaukee Cannibal or the Milwaukee Monster
2. 17 males
3. Borderline personality disorder (BPD), schizotypal personality disorder (StPD), and a psychotic disorder
4. 1992
5. Steven Mark Hicks
6. Christopher Scarver
7. Ohio
8. He worked as a phlebotomist at the Milwaukee Blood Plasma Center and later as a mixer at the Ambrosia Chocolate Factory.
9. West Allis, Wisconsin, to live with his grandmother
10. He drilled holes in their skulls and injected hydrochloric acid or boiling water in an attempt to create a submissive state.

Randy Kraft

1. Scorecard Killer
2. California
3. U.S. Air Force
4. 1983
5. Sixteen
6. Strangulation
7. Many of his victims were found near freeways
8. Republican
9. 61
10. He was found guilty and sentenced to death
11. San Quentin State Prison
12. Jeff Seelig
13. Photographs of Loggins found in Kraft's possession
14. Randy Kraft's trial
15. Abrasions and debris suggesting multiple people carried bodies to dumping sites
16. A list of 61 coded victim names and photos of victims
17. Jeff Graves
18. Patrick Kearney and William Bonin

Robert Hansen

1. The Butcher Baker
2. At least seventeen women
3. 1983
4. 461 years
5. Estherville, Iowa
6. He was painfully shy, had a stutter, and suffered from severe acne.
7. 1957
8. Burning down a Pocahontas County school bus garage
9. Manic depression with periodic schizophrenic episodes
10. 1967
11. Two children
12. A Ruger Mini-14 rifle and hunting knives
13. Celia van Zanten
14. She escaped while Hansen was loading his airplane.
15. Her blue sneakers
16. Jewelry belonging to missing women and a .223-caliber Ruger Mini-14 rifle
17. Thirty-seven marks
18. John Douglas
19. He provided details about his victims in exchange for certain conditions, including serving his sentence in a federal prison.
20. Seventeen grave sites

Richard Cottingham

1. The Torso Killer and the Times Square Ripper
2. 18 murders
3. 2009
4. Computer operator
5. Three children
6. Handcuffs, leather gag, two slave collars, switchblade knife, replica pistols, prescription pills
7. Hasbrouck Heights Quality Inn
8. "You have to take it. The other girls did, you have to take it, too. You're a whore and you have to be punished."
9. Items belonging to several of his victims
10. He beat her, tortured her with a garden hose, and caused injuries to her face, breasts, vagina, and rectum
11. She was strangled and dumped in the Quality Inn parking lot in Hasbrouck Heights, New Jersey
12. His fingerprint was found on the handcuffs left on her body
13. Travel Lodge Motor Inn
14. He set her body on fire and left her breasts on the headboard of the bed
15. He drowned them in the bathtub after tying them up and raping them
16. 1967 murder of Mary Ann Della Sala
17. Montvale double-homicide of Lorraine Marie Kelly and Mary Ann Pryor
18. 2022
19. Mary Ann Della Sala

Randall Woodfield

1. The I-5 Killer or the I-5 Bandit
2. Linked to 18 murders, suspected of killing up to 44
3. Football, Green Bay Packers
4. During high school
5. At knifepoint
6. Cherie Ayers, October 1980
7. Life imprisonment plus 90 years
8. Oregon State Penitentiary
9. Otter Rock, Oregon; football
10. Three times
11. A fake beard and athletic tape across his nose
12. 1981; Chris Van Dyke

Larry Eyler

1. Interstate Killer and Highway Killer.
2. Between 1982 and 1984.
3. Stabbing and/or slashing.
4. His involvement in twenty further unsolved homicides.
5. AIDS-related complications.
6. Robert David Little.
7. Discarding them in fields close to major highways.
8. Daniel Bridges.
9. Kathleen Zellner.
10. Fingerprints on plastic bags used to dispose of Bridges' remains.

Francisco Guerrero Pérez

1. El Chalequero
2. 20
3. Mexico City
4. Shoemaker
5. By strangling or slitting their throats
6. Hatred of women and sexual dominance
7. Detective Francisco Chávez
8. The murder of Murcia Gallardo and the assault on Emilia
9. Death sentence, later changed to 20 years imprisonment by Porfirio Díaz
10. 1904
11. The murder of an elderly woman named Antonia
12. Witnesses including a young shepherd and two women who saw him cleaning off blood
13. Lecumberri Prison
14. Rejection by his mother during childhood
15. Likely from tuberculosis, typhoid, or a cerebral embolism

Javed Iqbal

1. His anger over perceived injustice by the police, especially related to his previous arrest for sodomy, and his desire to make 100 mothers suffer as he believed his mother had.
2. December 1999.
3. He dissolved their bodies in acid and emptied the remains into a local river.
4. Between 6 and 16 years old.
5. Bloodstains, a strangling chain, photos of the victims, and vats of acid with partially dissolved remains.
6. The death of his mother after his arrest and decline in social status.
7. He was found hanged in his cell, though autopsies suggested he had been beaten before death.
8. The offices of the Daily Jang newspaper.
9. Death by strangulation, followed by dismemberment and dissolving his body in acid.
10. "Javed Iqbal: The Untold Story of A Serial Killer," released on 2 June 2023.

Mikhail Popkov

1. "The Werewolf" and "the Angarsk Maniac"
2. 86 murders
3. Angarsk, Irkutsk, and Vladivostok
4. Police officer and security guard
5. 2015
6. Tracks from a Lada 4x4 vehicle used by law enforcement
7. He wanted to "cleanse the streets of prostitutes"
8. Knives, axes, baseball bats, and screwdrivers
9. 2018
10. Two additional killings
11. His wife
12. 9 years and 8 months
13. 1964
14. Capital punishment moratorium
15. "The Wednesday Murderer"

Daniel Camargo Barbosa

1. 22 January 1930
2. At least 72
3. Geovanny Noguera, nephew of one of his victims
4. 116
5. Due to her fertility problems, she was abusive and humiliated him.
6. 1958, for petty theft
7. Esperanza
8. The kidnapping, rape, and murder of a 9-year-old girl
9. Gorgona Island
10. In a primitive boat after studying the ocean currents
11. Quito, Ecuador
12. *Crime and Punishment* by Dostoyevsky
13. 16 years
14. Pedro Alonso López
15. 64 years old

Pedro Rodrigues Filho

1. 29 October 1954
2. Pedrinho Matador (Lil' Petey Killer)
3. 14 years old
4. The murder of his pregnant girlfriend
5. 71 murders
6. 2007
7. Inciting riot and deprivation of liberty
8. Pedrinho EX Matador
9. Dexter Morgan
10. He was shot and killed by two men on 5 March 2023

Hoshang Amini

1. The Ghost of the Qanat Wells
2. Varamin
3. 67
4. Asghar the Murderer
5. Vulnerable young boys (but also adult men and women)
6. Dumping them in wells after decapitation
7. Asghar the Murderer
8. The body of an unidentified German man
9. He was found hiding in a chest at his sister's house
10. The Felt Hat Killer
11. Parviz Yahaghi
12. 1963
13. "Killing me will not solve anything. Go find the cause. You have so many doctors. There are 3,000 people like me in Tehran. I am not afraid."
14. "The Last Execution" by Zakaria Hashemi

Yang Xinhai

1. July 17, 1968
2. Yang Zhiya and Yang Liu
3. 67 murders and 23 rapes
4. "Monster Killer"
5. 1985
6. Attempted rape
7. Between 1999 and 2003
8. Anhui, Hebei, Henan, and Shandong
9. Axes, hammers, and shovels
10. He wore new clothes and large shoes
11. He killed a father and a six-year-old girl, raped the pregnant woman, but she survived with serious head injuries
12. November 3, 2003
13. February 1, 2004
14. Firing squad
15. Revenge against society due to a breakup
16. Enjoyment of robbery, rape, and murder
17. He stated, "When I killed people I had a desire. This inspired me to kill more. I don't care whether they deserve to live or not. It is none of my concern … Society is not my concern."

Samuel Little

1. 93
2. Violent Criminal Apprehension Program
3. Reynolds, Georgia
4. Cemetery worker
5. Mississippi
6. 2012
7. Four life sentences
8. 2018
9. Strangulation
10. Confessing to cold case murders
11. 2020, in a Los Angeles County hospital
12. 60 murders
13. Orelia Dorsey
14. Eight murders
15. 2014

William Unek

1. Police constable
2. 57 people
3. Belgian Congo
4. Two women and a child
5. His wife
6. Nine days
7. $350
8. Iyumbu ben Ikumbu
9. A smoke bomb

Mohammed Bijeh

1. Iranian
2. 54 young boys
3. June 2002 to September 2004
4. 100 lashes followed by execution
5. 8 to 15 years old
6. He wanted to take revenge on the community because of his suffering in childhood, including being raped and losing his mother early.
7. 11 years old
8. His mother died when he was 4, and he was beaten and chained by his father, forced to leave school, and raped multiple times.
9. 24 September 2004
10. He would kill 100 children
11. Pakdasht
12. About 5,000 people
13. A relative of one of the victims
14. He was hoisted by a crane with a rope around his neck until he died.

Andrei Chikatilo

1. The Butcher of Rostov or the Rostov Ripper
2. 1978
3. Fifty-six
4. Fifty-two
5. By gunshot
6. Yabluchne, Ukraine
7. The forced collectivization famine caused by Joseph Stalin
8. World War II
9. That Stepan had been kidnapped and cannibalized by starving neighbors
10. Chronic impotence
11. Chairman
12. Communications technician
13. Rostov-on-Don
14. Through stabbing and mutilating his victims
15. 1984
16. A semen test showed his semen type was different from his blood type
17. He would often promise assistance or offer food, candy, or other items of interest
18. He created a psychological profile and later helped to elicit Chikatilo's confession
19. That the image of a murderer is left imprinted on the eyes of the victim
20. Rostov

Anatoly Onoprienko

1. The Beast of Ukraine (also accepted: The Terminator, Citizen O)
2. Fifty-two people
3. Lasky, Zhytomyr Oblast, Ukrainian SSR, Soviet Union
4. Four years old
5. Inner voices
6. 1989
7. Ten people (two adults and eight children)
8. A sawed-off shotgun (TOZ-34)
9. The Zaichenko family
10. Four people
11. They were shot and killed in their home, and the home was set ablaze
12. Shot the father and son, and mauled the mother and daughter with a hammer
13. Set them alight to cover the evidence
14. Yury Mozola
15. 1996
16. It was commuted to life imprisonment
17. 54 years old

Florisvaldo de Oliveira

1. Cabo Bruno
2. 1958
3. São Paulo
4. It was a provocation from his friends, comparing him to a local alcoholic named Bruno.
5. The 1980s
6. More than 50
7. He pretended to be dead after being shot.
8. Chevrolet Chevette, Ford Maverick, and Chevrolet Impala
9. 1983
10. One murder initially, later admitting to about 20.
11. 113 years
12. Three times
13. He became a pastor in the ecumenical chapel.
14. 2009
15. He was granted freedom after 27 years' imprisonment.
16. 27 years
17. Between 18 and 20 shots
18. A religious service in Aparecida
19. A .40 Smith & Wesson and a .38 Colt automatic pistol
20. They auctioned them off to restart their lives elsewhere.

Gary Ridgway

1. The Green River Killer
2. 48 murders
3. Sex workers and women in vulnerable circumstances
4. Strangulation
5. Forested and overgrown areas in King County, Washington
6. The Green River Killer
7. DNA profiling
8. 2001
9. Spray painter at the Kenworth truck factory
10. He agreed to disclose the locations of missing women in exchange for avoiding the death penalty.
11. 48 life sentences without the possibility of parole
12. Born February 18, 1949, in Salt Lake City, Utah
13. Conflicted feelings of anger and sexual attraction towards her
14. Dyslexia
15. Stabbed a six-year-old boy
16. It ended in divorce
17. Proselytizing, reading the Bible aloud, and insisting on strict religious observance
18. Three
19. Bundy suggested Ridgway returned to the dump sites to have sex with the bodies.
20. 1984

21. 48 murders

22. Oregon

23. Having sex with the deceased victims reduced his need for new victims.

24. 48 life sentences without the possibility of parole

25. Washington State Penitentiary

Alexander Pichushkin

1. The Chessboard Killer
2. At least forty-nine people, possibly as many as sixty
3. 2007
4. Bitsa Park
5. Falling backward off a swing and being struck in the forehead
6. His maternal grandfather
7. Chess
8. Mikhail Odïtchuk
9. A hammer
10. Sticks or an empty vodka bottle
11. God
12. Andrei Chikatilo
13. Sixty-four squares (chessboard)
14. Bitsa Park
15. A Moscow Metro ticket and surveillance footage
16. Forty-nine murders
17. Solitary confinement
18. Polar Owl

Ahmad Suradji

1. Dukun AS, Nasib Klewang, and Datuk Maringgi
2. 42
3. 1986 to 1997
4. By strangling them after burying them up to their waists
5. A sugarcane field
6. Medan
7. Cattle breeder and dukun (shaman)
8. To murder 72 women as part of a black magic ritual
9. He thought it would take too long to wait for natural deaths
10. Sri Kemala Dewi
11. 42
12. Their saliva
13. His three wives, including Tumini
14. 11 December 1997
15. He was found guilty and sentenced to death
16. By firing squad on 10 July 2008

Raman Raghav

1. Sindhi Talwai, Anna, Thambi, Veluswami
2. Mid-1960s (first round in 1965–1966, second round in 1968)
3. 19 people (9 died)
4. A hard, blunt object
5. Sub-inspector Alex Fialho
6. 41 murders
7. Chronic paranoid schizophrenia
8. Life imprisonment due to mental illness
9. Sassoon Hospital
10. Reduced from death to life imprisonment

Moses Sithole

1. The ABC Murders
2. 37 women and one toddler
3. Mangaung Correctional Centre in Bloemfontein
4. His father died and his mother abandoned the family
5. Seven years
6. Youth Against Human Abuse
7. Strangling them with their underwear
8. President Nelson Mandela
9. 1997
10. 2,410 years
11. 963 years old
12. HIV and tuberculosis (TB)

Gennady Mikhasevich

1. Soviet (Byelorussian SSR).
2. At least 36 women.
3. 1971.
4. His girlfriend left him and married someone else.
5. Strangulation or smothering.
6. A red Zaporozhets.
7. 'Patriots of Vitebsk.'
8. 556,000 samples.
9. December 1985.
10. He was sentenced to death and executed by firing squad.

Vera Renczi

1. The Black Widow, Mrs. Poison, or Chatelaine of Berkerekul
2. 35 individuals
3. Arsenic
4. Karl Schick, a wealthy Austrian banker
5. She claimed he had abandoned her and later died in a car accident
6. 13 years old
7. She had a pathological desire for constant male companionship and a jealous nature
8. Running away from home with numerous older boyfriends
9. After receiving a tip from Milorad's wife and searching her chateau
10. 35 coffins
11. She suspected her victims of being unfaithful or losing interest in her
12. She liked to sit surrounded by the coffins of her former lovers
13. Yugoslavia did not execute women at the time
14. 1960
15. The Amy Archer-Gilligan case
16. *Deadly Women*

Fernando Hernández Leyva

1. 1964
2. 33 counts of murder
3. Around 100 murders
4. 137 murders
5. 13 years
6. Twice
7. 1999
8. By hanging himself
9. His weight caused the rope to break
10. 4 states
11. "Pancho López"
12. He claimed he was beaten and threatened by bailiffs
13. The authorities
14. Morelos
15. 2049

John Wayne Gacy

1. "The Killer Clown"
2. At least 33 victims
3. In the crawl space of his house
4. 1968
5. The investigation into the disappearance of Robert Piest
6. By asphyxiation or strangulation with a garrote
7. A bucket of KFC, french fries, fried shrimp, strawberries, and a Diet Coke
8. Illinois
9. A heart condition
10. 14 years
11. Because he performed as a clown at public events while committing his murders
12. 1994
13. His father was abusive, both verbally and physically
14. He used a pretext of demonstrating a magic trick with handcuffs
15. The investigation into the disappearance of Robert Piest
16. Lethal injection
17. He was involved in politics and was known for his charitable work as a clown
18. Paranoid schizophrenia with multiple personalities
19. He disposed of bodies in the Des Plaines River
20. Police badges, handcuffs, pornographic films, a syringe, and other suspicious items were found.

Ali Asghar Borujerdi

1. Asghar the Murderer (Asghar-e Ghatel)
2. Iraq and Iran
3. 33 (25 in Iraq, 8 in Iran)
4. 14 years old
5. Male teens and children
6. His father was a bandit who killed over 40 civilians, and his grandfather was also a bandit.
7. Baghdad
8. Tehran
9. They noticed bloody clothes and a bloody knife in his possession.
10. He was executed by hanging on July 6, 1934.
11. 8 murders in Iran
12. He believed they were "enemies of society" and that they would become thieves as they grew up.

Vasili Komaroff

1. Vasili Terentevich Petrov
2. 33 people
3. Horse trader
4. 1921
5. Hammer or slitting the throat
6. Hidden around the house, buried underground, or dumped in the Moscow River
7. His wife, Sophia
8. The discovery of a body under a stack of hay in his stable
9. Three times
10. 1923
11. "An awfully easy job"
12. 26 Shabolovka Street
13. Suspicion of illegal alcohol
14. Robbery
15. 6 bodies
16. He was found sane, but recognized as an alcoholic degenerate and psychopath

Radik Tagirov

1. Volga Maniac
2. Tatarstan
3. Locksmithing
4. 31
5. 75 to 90 years old
6. Pretending to be an employee of a utility company or social service
7. Strangulation with improvised items or his hands
8. Kazan
9. The alleged perpetrator's image at the entrance of one of the victims' homes
10. 1 million rubles
11. 2017
12. DNA evidence and shoe prints
13. At least 25
14. October 2022
15. Life in prison

Karl Denke

1. The Cannibal of Münsterberg and the Forgotten Cannibal
2. 1903
3. Farming
4. Leather goods and boneless meat
5. Cross-bearer and organist
6. Ida Launer
7. He was wrongfully convicted of her murder and released years later when the truth was revealed.
8. He sold their flesh as pickled meat, advertising it as pork.
9. Rochus Pawlick
10. The testimony of a homeless drifter named Vincenz Olivier, who escaped after Denke tried to kill him.
11. He hanged himself in his cell with a handkerchief or shoelace.
12. Human flesh in brine, human bones, fat, and items made from human skin.
13. 30 victims
14. As high as 42 or even more
15. His motives, exact methods, and the total number of his victims remain unknown.

Monster of the Mangones

1. The Monster of the Mangones
2. Between 30 and 38
3. Inserting needles into the heart and thorax, assaults, rapes, torture, and drawing blood with syringes
4. Reinfeld's syndrome
5. November 5, 1963
6. Eyeballs
7. They claimed the bodies were taken from cemeteries and scattered around Cali
8. Between April and late 1964
9. Between 30 and 38
10. *Pura sangre*, directed by Luis Ospina
11. He suffers from a condition that requires him to ingest blood in order to survive

Milton Sipalo

1. The Lusaka Strangler.
2. 29 women and girls.
3. He was recognized by one of his surviving victims at a bus station.
4. He lured victims from public places, raped, and strangled them, leaving their bodies in open spaces.
5. Many victims had strange mucus or foam oozing from their noses, possibly from chemical use.
6. All of his victims were Lozi or spoke Lozi.
7. "Operation Rosemary."
8. Patrols were set up, undercover female detectives were planted, and a reward was offered.
9. They planted undercover Lozi-speaking female detectives at bus terminals.
10. She managed to kick her attacker off of her.
11. The attacker spoke with a Lozi accent, and witnesses saw him in a military uniform.
12. The woman has never been identified, and it is unknown whether she survived or became another victim.
13. She recognized him by the wristwatch he had stolen from her during her attack.
14. Items belonging to several of his victims.
15. He admitted, "If they can pick me from the line of others, then I am the one who tried to kill them."

16. He escaped from police custody and jumped from the roof of a police station, killing himself.

Zhang Jun

1. 1966
2. 22 stores
3. 28 people
4. 5.36 million yuan
5. Due to poverty
6. Sentenced to labor reform
7. 455,000 yuan
8. December 25, 1996
9. Two people killed, 1.372 million yuan in jewelry stolen
10. Two people killed
11. 2.634 million yuan in gold jewelry
12. The president of the bank, killing two people and stealing 16,000 yuan
13. Seven people
14. The robbery was unsuccessful, and Zhang accidentally injured his companion, leading to his death.
15. He killed his companion and fled to Guangxi.
16. A military hand grenade
17. Wen Qiang, deputy director of the Chongqing Municipal Public Security Bureau
18. April 14, 2001
19. May 20, 2001

Mariam Soulakiotis

1. Marina Soulakiotou
2. "Mother Rasputin"
3. Fourteen years
4. Panagia Pefkovounogiatrissa Monastery
5. December 1950
6. By convincing wealthy women to join the convent, torturing them, and embezzling their fortunes
7. More than 100
8. The FBI
9. She died in Averoff Prison
10. 177
11. He argued it was due to there being no legal person behind the monastery
12. World War II
13. Between Keratea and Kaki Thalassa in East Attica
14. Saint Matthew
15. The Matthewite Old Calendarist sect
16. Eighty-five
17. A serial killer
18. On the grounds of the Panagia Pefkovounogiatrissa Monastery

Cedric Maake

1. Plumber
2. Johannesburg
3. 1996
4. He committed most of his murders in the Wemmer Pan area of Johannesburg.
5. Hammers, rocks, and firearms
6. 27
7. They created two separate profiles, one for the Wemmer Pan murders and another for the Hammer murders.
8. Geographic Information Systems (GIS) and crime mapping technology
9. Patrick Mokwena
10. 27 life sentences
11. 114 charges
12. 1,340 years

Robert Pickton

1. Pig farmer
2. Between 1995 and 2001
3. 49 murders
4. Six counts
5. Life in prison with no possibility of parole for 25 years
6. The crisis of missing and murdered Indigenous women
7. Missing Women Commission of Inquiry
8. The Pickton pig farm
9. Piggy's Palace
10. Wendy Lynn Eistetter
11. David Pickton
12. They were stayed (dismissed)
13. He may have ground up human flesh and mixed it with pork
14. Six counts
15. Clothes and rubber boots
16. 2012
17. *Da Vinci's Inquest*
18. *Pig Killer*
19. A T-shirt with the caricature "Pickton Farms" and "Over 50 flavors of hookery smoked bacon"

Bruce George Peter Lee

1. Peter George Dinsdale.
2. 26 counts.
3. A fire broke out at the front of a house on Selby Street, leading to the deaths of three children.
4. He rescued his mother by pushing her out of an upstairs window.
5. Tredget had some sexual contact with Charles and had become infatuated with Charles' sister.
6. A total of 11 acts of arson and 26 counts of manslaughter (he later confessed to nine additional fatal fires).
7. The inquiry concluded the fire was accidental and not caused by Tredget, leading to the quashing of his manslaughter convictions on appeal.
8. Park Lane Special Hospital in Liverpool.
9. In 1979.
10. He launched a libel action after the paper suggested Tredget's statements were not entirely voluntary.

The Stoneman

1. Thirteen murders
2. Mumbai and Calcutta
3. Victims were killed by crushing their heads with a stone weighing up to 30 kg
4. Whether the murders were committed by the same person or multiple individuals
5. The Mumbai Police
6. He was unable to get a good look at the attacker due to dim lighting
7. The killings suddenly stopped, and the case remains unsolved
8. The suspects were released due to lack of evidence, and the crimes remain unsolved
9. Guwahati in 2009
10. *The Stoneman Murders*
11. 40% fact, 60% fiction
12. *Baishe Srabon*

Juan Corona

1. California
2. 25 murders
3. Bodies of migrant farm workers
4. Electroconvulsive therapy
5. Meat receipts and deposit slips bearing his name, blood-stained items in his home, and a work ledger
6. 25 victims
7. Richard Hawk
8. 25 counts
9. He was found guilty again on all counts
10. His work ledger

Fritz Haarmann

1. The Butcher of Hanover, the Vampire of Hanover, the Wolf Man
2. Hanover
3. 24 of 27
4. Biting into or through their throats
5. He was a quiet, effeminate child who preferred playing with dolls and doing needlework.
6. He discharged himself from the military and briefly worked in his father's cigar factory.
7. He escaped with apparent assistance from his mother and fled to Switzerland.
8. Haarmann briefly worked as an insurance salesman.
9. Hans Grans
10. Friedel Rothe
11. The Leine River
12. That he sold it on the black market as pork or horse meat.
13. He became an informant to redirect police attention from his own criminal activities.
14. Poverty, crime, and black market trading.
15. Biting into or through his victims' Adam's apple.
16. Grans was accused of inciting some of the murders and coveting the victims' possessions.
17. In a communal grave at Stöckener Cemetery.
18. He was beheaded by guillotine.

19. "Somewhere between 50 and 70."

20. He claimed it was an irresistible urge triggered by sexual ecstasy.

21. It was examined for traces of disease and later cremated.

22. Homophobia and legal issues regarding homosexuality.

23. Carl Gröpler

24. 1928

Béla Kiss

1. Tinsmith
2. 24 bodies
3. The landlord poked a hole in one of the barrels, releasing a terrible stench
4. Gasoline for rationing
5. He was conscripted to war
6. Letters from 74 women, a photo album, books on poisons and strangulation
7. They were usually middle-aged women with no nearby relatives
8. Vampirism
9. Kiss fled, leaving the body of another soldier in his bed
10. Hoffman
11. New York City, 1932, near Times Square

Yvan Keller

1. 13 December 1960, Wittenheim, Haut-Rhin
2. The Pillow Killer
3. Around 150
4. He worked in Alsace's potash mines
5. Age 17, for stealing antiques
6. A landscape gardening company named Alsa-Jardin
7. Marina
8. He put a gun in the man's mouth and threatened him
9. He suffocated them in their beds and then remade the bed to perfection
10. Three times
11. He hung himself at the Mulhouse High Court

Ronald Dominique

1. The Bayou Strangler
2. At least 23 people
3. January 9, 1964
4. Louisiana
5. 1997 to 2006
6. September 23, 2008
7. The Federal Bureau of Investigation (FBI)
8. Poor laborers
9. He struggled with low-skilled jobs and lived off relatives
10. Sexual harassment committed via telephone
11. The prosecutor's office couldn't locate the alleged victim
12. He was often looked down upon and sometimes dressed as Patti LaBelle
13. He lured them with offers of alcohol, drugs, housing, or group sex
14. David Mitchell
15. Accidental drowning
16. Strangulation
17. St. Charles Parish
18. Christopher Sutterfield
19. A man named Ricky Wallace reported Dominique's suspicious behavior
20. A homeless shelter
21. 23 murders
22. He didn't want to serve prison time again
23. By pleading guilty to all charges

24. Louisiana State Penitentiary in Angola

Juan Fernando Hermosa

1. 1976
2. Niño del Terror
3. 15 years old
4. 22 murders
5. A 9mm pistol
6. Grupo de Intervención y Rescate (GIR)
7. During the shootout at Hermosa's residence
8. 15 years old
9. Four years imprisonment
10. A pistol
11. He escaped with ten young boys after killing a policeman
12. He was found dead, disfigured and tortured on the banks of the Aguarico River

Earle Nelson

1. The Gorilla Man, the Gorilla Killer, and the Dark Strangler.
2. San Francisco and Portland, Oregon.
3. Posing as a mild-mannered drifter to rent rooms from landladies, then strangling and raping them.
4. Strangulation.
5. Lola Cowan, whose body was mutilated.
6. 22 murders and 22 other attacks.
7. Syphilis.
8. Age 7, and he sustained a head injury from a bicycling accident at age 10.
9. Napa State Mental Hospital.
10. 1927, and he was executed in Canada.
11. *Shadow of a Doubt.*
12. He compulsively quoted Biblical passages and obsessed over the Book of Revelation.
13. Guilty of murder, sentenced to death by hanging.
14. A passage from the Book of Proverbs.
15. "I forgive those who have wronged me."

Patrick Kearney

1. The Trash Bag Killer and The Freeway Killer
2. A minimum of twenty-one
3. Engineer for Hughes Aircraft
4. 1962
5. George
6. 1974
7. He shot them in the temple with a .22 pistol
8. Ronald Dean Smith, age 5
9. John Otis LaMay
10. 28 murders
11. Twenty-one life sentences

William Bonin

1. The Freeway Killer
2. He was convicted of 14 murders and confessed to 21.
3. Thomas Glen Lundgren
4. Strangulation with a tire iron or his victims' own T-shirts
5. Vernon Butts was an accomplice in several of Bonin's murders, helping him abduct, torture, and kill victims.
6. San Quentin State Prison, lethal injection
7. 121
8. He was sexually assaulted by an older boy.
9. His mother
10. His misanthropic beliefs and criminal behavior
11. He recited what he thought psychiatrists wanted to hear to manipulate them into granting early release.
12. A Ford Econoline van, with the door handles removed to prevent escape
13. A tip from an acquaintance, William Pugh, who knew about Bonin's criminal methods
14. Steven Jay Wells, with help from James Munro
15. 14 years
16. That he did not pursue his passion for bowling
17. The Freeway Killer
18. He opposed it, calling it wrong.
19. Donald Ray Hyden
20. His childhood abuse and dysfunctional upbringing